THE AFTER SESSION WORKBOOK

THE AFTER SESSION WORKBOOK

12 Real-World Therapy Sessions on Emotional Reconciliation

PHILLIP J. LEWIS

SoulRebel

CONTENTS

I
DEDICATION   1

II
INTRODUCTION   3

  1 Just Being   6

  2 Obligation vs. Motivation   21

  3 Hurt a Little   28

  4 Therapists Are Like Shoes   44

  5 Our Operating Systems, and Our Apps   65

  6 Acknowledge Your Feelings, Before It's Too Late.   81

  7 Self-Attunement   99

  8 Self-Love = Revolution   115

  9 Shifting Worlds   128

  10 Freedom and Free Will   148

  11 How to Confront Fear?   169

  12 Faith, Belief, and Knowing   189

III

ACKNOWLEDGMENTS 215

About The Author 217

Edited by Cory Myer
Cover Art by Donavon Brutus

Copyright © 2024 by Phillip J. Lewis

All rights reserved. No part of this book may be reproduced in any manner whatsoever without written permission except in the case of brief quotations embodied in critical articles and reviews.

First Printing, 2024

Dedication

This workbook honors everyone who seeks emotional reconciliation. Wherever you are on your journey, I'm proud of you for simply picking up this book. We are all navigating challenges – some large and some small. Often, the solutions lie within our own unwavering self-acceptance and compassion. Love propels the most genuine transformations. In nurturing our souls, we take on the work and responsibility of shaping our lives for the better. That process starts with unconditional positive self-regard. Getting there isn't easy, but it provides the safest way to navigate life's messy twists and turns. If you're committed to being better to yourself, this book is dedicated to you.

UNDERSTANDING OF EMOTIONAL RECONCILIATION:

I believe that Emotional Reconciliation is any process we use to resolve and come to terms with past emotional conflicts, traumas, or misunderstandings, leading to a state of inner peace and understanding.

Even if the emotional and tangible realities do not match, alignment is not a part of the process but can be helpful. Authenticity, confronting ourselves, and learning from our feelings are the key aspects of the reconciliation process. Accepting ourselves and our emotions as they come is where the lesson lies and the possibility of positively changing what we feel about ourselves and our experiences.

This process involves acknowledging and accepting one's feelings and experiences, and those of others involved, to heal emotional wounds and mend relationships. Emotional reconciliation can occur within oneself, through reconciling one's feelings and thoughts about past events, or between individuals, where parties work through conflicts or hurt feelings to restore harmony and understanding in their relationship. This process often requires empathy, communication, forgiveness, and a willingness to move past grievances to achieve a healthier emotional state and interpersonal dynamics.

Empathy, communication, forgiveness, and willingness to move forward starts with the self, and the more we do this for ourselves, the easier it is to reconcile with others.

Introduction

Throughout my therapeutic career, and while writing this, I have often wondered if I should even be giving others advice. There were voices of doubt, given all I have been through, as a natural part of the human experience, all that I intentionally put myself through, as a response to the pain I was exposed to, and all the things I may do in the future, as a result of future pain. These past, present, and possible future experiences created a narrative about me and my clinical practice, which, of course, changes depending on how I feel about myself professionally and personally.

Clients never genuinely know who their therapist is. They see us for 45-60 minutes in our office. We give insights, explain the science behind behaviors and responses, and offer the support (yes, sometimes love) needed to get through whatever brought them into the office to begin with.

That's all the information our clients get. With it, they create pictures and ideas of who we are in their minds. This is what the mind does. It creates narratives based on the information it has. Of course, that information tells an incomplete story.

If the therapist is always on time, quick-witted, ready with an answer, gives examples of coping skills, shows resolve, and gives solutions to life's most complex challenges, how could our clients *not* assume this is how we always are? We must be the same outside of the office, right?

Therapists with complete families have high emotional intelligence and regularly ask for our needs to be met without apprehension or concern that someone won't meet them. Of course, that's not reality. We therapists are human.

This workbook is the product of my three-year therapeutic journey. The stories, lessons, practice applications, and pain on these pages reflect my processing of the situations and emotions presented by my clients. Thank you for being vulnerable and trusting me if you're one of them. Despite everything, you've had the strength to challenge concepts, do the difficult work, pick yourself up, and pursue your desired life.

I have healed myself through you, and this book is my way of saying thank you.

A client asked if I could write down or record our sessions to share later, so I began blogging. She inspired my first piece, "*Freedom and Free Will.*" She didn't know it at the time, but while I was challenging her throughout our therapeutic process together, I was also struggling with a similar challenge in my personal life. Each time she completed the homework, had a challenging conversation with family, and stuck by what she wanted in a partner, she gave me the courage to do the same. She thought I was leading her, but really, she was leading me. I am continually amazed by clients' trust in us as therapists. They believe in our advice, take the risk of putting it into action, and return to therapy, affirming completion, change, and expressing happiness for accepting the mission. Watching my clients do the work and see it through to completion has always helped me do the same in my own life.

This book is an anthology of pain, self-love, discovery, and understanding. Still, it is also a social experiment, where we will test the capacity to love ourselves, find motivations for change, go with what might not have been tested or proven, and survive to tell the story—at the same time, finding positive, conducive, and lasting change.

Each chapter contains four parts:

1. An exploration of the individual and their experience ("The Client")
2. My takeaways as a therapist ("The After Session")
3. A space to have a *Practice Reflective Dialogue*, a chance to have a conversation with yourself about the topic
4. A reflective journal exercise for the week

These thought exercises helped my clients – and me – navigate our challenges and reach the finish line. I hope they will help you do the same. If you can see the benefit, I am happy for you; if you are beyond the work in this book, I'm even happier.

Take what you need, leave the rest, and be good to yourself.

To those I've worked with and will work with someday, you aren't just my clients. You've been *my* therapist the whole time. For that, I thank you!

CHAPTER 1

Just Being

William:

William was an extraordinary individual, though he seemed oblivious to his light.

In a world rife with systemic racism and bias, William carried an added burden. His anxiety and depression, he initially assumed, were the product of a genetic predisposition. His father was seen as unpredictable, volatile, and self-serving. William's mother, although saint-like, was consistently preoccupied, and her love for him stretched thin due to her constant busyness and struggle to maintain a home. In pursuit of this thinly spread affection, William spent his formative years ensuring he didn't become a statistic; he began trying to accomplish, to gain the love and attention William had been missing, basing his worth and value on what he could achieve. Unfortunately, the highlights of achievement in childhood were all his parents had the emotional capacity to pay attention to. So this taught him that love, affection, care, and concern only came through external accomplishments and ensuring he always did well. He signed up for the military, excelled academically, and, during our initial session, shared a series of achievements and trials that had shaped the man he'd become.

Yet, he was perplexed by his ongoing struggle with anxiety, which had begun to interfere with his relationships and job performance.

In our first meeting, I raised a fundamental question:

"Are you tired of being a collateral person?"

He had spent the majority of his life becoming someone he was expected to be, striving to defy stereotypes, and resisting the stigmas associated with his race. This pursuit led him to favor what he perceived as *'right'* over what he felt was emotionally resonant or aligned with his desires and genuine self-understanding. William also believed that his inherent worth was conditional to what he did or what was in his environment, not who he was or what he felt to be true about who he was (the things on the inside).

As a Black man, he was particularly vulnerable to microaggressions and systemic biases that are deeply embedded in our society. This constant pressure to prove himself and avoid fitting into negative stereotypes intensified his anxiety and created a barrier preventing him from "just being."

William found himself living as a collateral individual – a man shaped more by the expectations of his family and society rather than by his own wants and needs. His ongoing struggle to determine his true self fueled his anxiety, and symptoms contributed to the internal dialogue that measured him against everything and everyone around him – a constant belief of not being good enough – increasing his depression.

Our work together aimed to help William see this pattern and begin detaching his identity from the societal pressures and stereotypes that had constrained him. We sought to introduce him to the concept of "just being." This meant granting himself the freedom to explore his emotions, desires, and aspirations without the heavy load of societal expectations or the fear of conforming to stereotypes.

We employed various therapeutic techniques, practiced mindfulness, and encouraged self-compassion exercises. These activities were designed to foster a sense of self-love and authenticity within William. In addition to the traditional therapeutic objectives, we also discussed how challenging these social constructs are, personally and macro-level.

A part of our work was detaching old concepts, rebuilding a belief of self that matches his inherent worth, and finding ways to dismantle, or at least safely challenge, and remove the systemic factors that framed his way of thinking in the first place. Gradually, he shed his collateral identity, becoming a more authentic version of himself. This journey, though filled with challenging introspection, also allowed for growing acceptance and a realization of his innate worth.

With every step, William was healing and discovering the remarkable individual he had always been – hidden beneath layers of expectations and personal anxieties. The process was not just about therapy. It was an awakening to his genuine self, unfettered by what the world had tried to impose on him.

The After Session:

Sometimes, in therapy sessions, someone will apologize for simply being human and for expressing human emotions. When discussing complex topics, they might cry...and apologize. When expressing frustration in a relationship, they might get angry...and apologize. When recalling a story from childhood, they might get anxious, shut down...and apologize.

The number one rule in my office is this:

<u>We NEVER apologize for how we feel</u>.

How we respond to a feeling, especially if it's negative, may call for an apology but not for *expressing* or *feeling* an emotion. This is a difficult rule because it goes against the norms and expectations of the world around us. Our society disincentivizes the free expression of our feelings and autonomy within the human experience and restricts the exploration of the human experience for some. Our society has different rules that are dependent on who you are, your social and economic status, sex, race, and several other things that are seen as distinct but only paid attention to when there is the opportunity to oppress or control.

Creating social constructs to disadvantage others physically, economically, and emotionally, not because they are inferior, but because of the fear that what distinguishes some might be an advantage (but this is a discussion for another book).

Outside of a therapeutic setting, we are rarely encouraged to explore the full depths of our emotions. So, when we do, we tend to apologize and correct ourselves. How many of us have asked a friend to hold space for us and started with, *"I'm sorry, but I just need to vent."* Or even in a therapist's office, a place specifically designed as a haven for free expression and exploration of feelings, how many of us have turned and apologized to our therapist for whatever we're emoting?

I find that this usually occurs when someone no longer restrains themselves and is – what I call – *just being*. We often think we need permission to *"just be."* If we aren't first granted permission by a loved one, or in this case, a therapist, we apologize, then snap back into restrictive mode and realize we've been emoting – existing – freely.

I require most of those I work with to ask themselves these questions when processing this topic:

1. Am I merely collateral to all the restrictions and expectations of the world, and what does society project onto me that I take as a standard for myself?
2. Am I the product of the experiences I've survived or enjoyed?
3. Am I someone who shows up exactly as the person I want to be?

Far too often, almost every time, these apologies come from men and women in positions of authority – whether professionally or in their households, that are traditionally reserved for people who do not look like them. Most believe that, as a Black man, "I can't be too masculine because being a strong Black man in the wrong spaces might impact my physical safety." Or "If I'm not masculine enough, my emotional safety will be at risk." "I can't be the statistic." "I must meet this standard." And so on.

Given society's rules and restrictions on how we can display our emotions, it's no wonder people have trouble reconciling them with how to behave in the world.

I see women struggle with the burden of assuming roles that the world says aren't traditionally for them. They apologize for providing their expertise – using their brilliance to save us all – and then apologize for being the savior. They can't be too bright, too strong, too this or too that. They must navigate the world under the pressure of what society says they *should* be while being strong enough to clean up the mess of broken men.

This dynamic can complicate anyone's growth or development. So, what can we do? It starts with providing ourselves and others with a space for self-exploration. If we are to learn and grow as people, we must allow for emotional reconciliation and expression. We must cultivate more spaces to embrace the human condition – spaces to *just be*.

REDISCOVERING AUTHENTICITY BEYOND SOCIETAL SCRIPTS

William's story is a compelling narrative of personal awakening and resistance against the constraints of ingrained social roles and systemic oppression. His evolution from a "collateral person" to an individual embodying his authentic self underscores a broader dialogue about identity, acceptance, and the human right to emotional freedom.

Throughout our sessions, William's unfolding story illuminated how deeply racial and societal constructs can infiltrate personal identity, dictating behaviors and expectations that often lead to psychological distress. The therapeutic process provided William with a sanctuary to dismantle these constructs, challenging the societal norms demanding he apologize for his very nature, emotions, and existence.

William's experience is a testament to the necessity of therapeutic spaces that advocate for emotional honesty without apology. This narrative extends an invitation to all individuals, particularly those from marginalized communities, to question and confront the societal scripts that shape their identities. It's a call to embrace vulnerability as a strength and to recognize that healing begins when one stops apologizing for one's feelings and starts understanding them as integral components of one's authentic self.

This story is not just about personal healing but also about societal reflection. It challenges us as a society to reconsider our roles in perpetuating stereotypes and restrictions that stifle individual growth and expression. It advocates for a more empathetic and inclusive understanding of emotional expression, devoid of preconceived notions tied to race, gender, or status.

As William's therapist, reflecting on our journey together reaffirms the transformative power of therapy – not merely as a tool for managing symptoms but as a profound engagement with the core of who we are. It is about creating a world where everyone can "just be," free from the apologies imposed by outdated and unjust societal expectations.

William's story encourages us all to continue the dialogue about emotional freedom and authenticity, creating environments that support the healing of individuals like William and the collective healing of our society. Through stories like his, we can begin to imagine and work towards a world where everyone can explore the full spectrum of their emotions without reservation or apology.

PRACTICE: **EXPLORING THE ART OF "JUST BEING"** DATE:
REFLECTIVE DIALOGUE

Contemplate the concept of "just being." This idea involves permitting yourself to exist as you are without the constant pressure to conform, achieve, or meet external expectations. Consider the following questions and allow yourself to engage in an internal or external dialogue with yourself:

What does "just being" mean to me personally & how are there any differences in how I usually live my day-to-day life?

_____
_____
_____
_____
_____

What internal and external barriers prevent me from allowing myself to *"just be?"*
(Family, work, insecurities, emotional vulnerability...)

_____
_____
_____
_____
_____

How might my life change if I allowed myself to "just be" more often?

_____
_____
_____
_____

WEEK 1 **EXPLORING THE ART OF "JUST BEING"** DAY 1
REFLECTIVE JOURNALING

For this practical exercise, we will integrate the concept of "just being" into everyday life through a reflective journaling exercise. Set aside 10-15 minutes at the end of each day this week to respond to the following prompts:

Describe a moment today when you felt you were *"just being."* How did it feel? What thoughts or emotions did it evoke?

_____

_____

_____

_____

_____

Were there moments today where you felt pressured to be something other than your authentic self?

_____

_____

How did you respond? How did it make you feel?

_____

_____

Write about one action you could take tomorrow to cultivate more moments of *"just being."*

_____

_____

_____

WEEK 1   **EXPLORING THE ART OF "JUST BEING"**   DAY 2
REFLECTIVE JOURNALING

For this practical exercise, we will integrate the concept of "just being" into everyday life through a reflective journaling exercise. Set aside 10-15 minutes at the end of each day this week to respond to the following prompts:

Describe a moment today when you felt you were *"just being."* How did it feel? What thoughts or emotions did it evoke?

___
___
___
___

Were there moments today where you felt pressured to be something other than your authentic self?

___
___

How did you respond? How did it make you feel?

___
___

Write about one action you could take tomorrow to cultivate more moments of *"just being."*

___
___
___

| WEEK 1 | **EXPLORING THE ART OF "JUST BEING"** | DAY 3 |

REFLECTIVE JOURNALING

For this practical exercise, we will integrate the concept of "just being" into everyday life through a reflective journaling exercise. Set aside 10-15 minutes at the end of each day this week to respond to the following prompts:

Describe a moment today when you felt you were *"just being."* How did it feel? What thoughts or emotions did it evoke?

___

Were there moments today where you felt pressured to be something other than your authentic self?

___

How did you respond? How did it make you feel?

___

Write about one action you could take tomorrow to cultivate more moments of *"just being."*

___

WEEK 1   **EXPLORING THE ART OF "JUST BEING"**   DAY 4
REFLECTIVE JOURNALING

For this practical exercise, we will integrate the concept of "just being" into everyday life through a reflective journaling exercise. Set aside 10-15 minutes at the end of each day this week to respond to the following prompts:

Describe a moment today when you felt you were *"just being."* How did it feel? What thoughts or emotions did it evoke?

_____

_____

_____

_____

Were there moments today where you felt pressured to be something other than your authentic self?

_____

_____

How did you respond? How did it make you feel?

_____

_____

_____

Write about one action you could take tomorrow to cultivate more moments of *"just being."*

_____

_____

_____

WEEK 1   **EXPLORING THE ART OF "JUST BEING"**   DAY 5
REFLECTIVE JOURNALING

For this practical exercise, we will integrate the concept of "just being" into everyday life through a reflective journaling exercise. Set aside 10-15 minutes at the end of each day this week to respond to the following prompts:

Describe a moment today when you felt you were *"just being."* How did it feel? What thoughts or emotions did it evoke?

_____
_____
_____
_____

Were there moments today where you felt pressured to be something other than your authentic self?

_____
_____
_____

How did you respond? How did it make you feel?

_____
_____
_____
_____

Write about one action you could take tomorrow to cultivate more moments of *"just being."*

_____
_____
_____
_____

WEEK 1   **EXPLORING THE ART OF "JUST BEING"**   DAY 6
REFLECTIVE JOURNALING

For this practical exercise, we will integrate the concept of "just being" into everyday life through a reflective journaling exercise. Set aside 10-15 minutes at the end of each day this week to respond to the following prompts:

Describe a moment today when you felt you were *"just being."* How did it feel? What thoughts or emotions did it evoke?

_____
_____
_____
_____

Were there moments today where you felt pressured to be something other than your authentic self?

_____
_____
_____

How did you respond? How did it make you feel?

_____
_____
_____

Write about one action you could take tomorrow to cultivate more moments of *"just being."*

_____
_____
_____

WEEK 1 — **EXPLORING THE ART OF "JUST BEING"** — DAY 7
REFLECTIVE JOURNALING

For this practical exercise, we will integrate the concept of "just being" into everyday life through a reflective journaling exercise. Set aside 10-15 minutes at the end of each day this week to respond to the following prompts:

Describe a moment today when you felt you were *"just being."* How did it feel? What thoughts or emotions did it evoke?

_____
_____
_____
_____

Were there moments today where you felt pressured to be something other than your authentic self?

_____
_____

How did you respond? How did it make you feel?

_____
_____
_____

Write about one action you could take tomorrow to cultivate more moments of *"just being."*

_____
_____
_____

CHAPTER 2

Obligation vs. Motivation

Shane:

Shane, a 35-year-old in a high-stress corporate job, walked into my office carrying the weight of ambition and societal expectations. Driven by a relentless need for achievement and advancement, he frequently put work above his personal well-being. Despite enjoying career success, Shane struggled to maintain a balanced lifestyle and manage stress effectively. This dynamic eventually led to moments of intense anxiety.

When Shane began therapy, the primary objective was to cultivate motivation for self-care and build distress tolerance. He recognized his unsustainable lifestyle and was eager to initiate positive changes. In addition to EMDR and psychoanalytic therapy, we focused on fostering motivation for mindfulness, regular physical activity, and healthier eating habits. Shane made noticeable progress, resulting in substantial improvements in both mental and physical health.

However, like what became evident for Shane, many individuals often feel the need to over-exert themselves to achieve and advance, and motivation fluctuates with the ups and downs of life. The pressures of work, personal matters, and everyday stressors often hampered Shane's commitment, causing him to revert to old, unhealthy habits.

Observing this pattern led to the introduction of the concept of self-obligation. We explored the idea that while motivation is vital, it can be fleeting. In contrast, obligation, mainly when directed towards oneself, can create a consistent sense of accountability. This accountability is crucial to maintaining personal health and well-being, even in the face of significant adversity.

Together, we identified areas where Shane struggled the most, such as saving money and managing stress without resorting to detrimental coping strategies. We devised strategies that fostered a sense of self-obligation, creating preventative barriers to impulsive spending and self-harming behaviors when faced with stress.

As Shane began to perceive these changes not merely as self-improvement goals but as *obligations* to his well-being, the transformations became more enduring. Although his motivation still varied, his commitment and obligation to himself ensured he stayed on course, maintaining progress despite low motivation.

In essence, Shane learned to obligate himself to himself, creating a sense of responsibility toward his well-being that superseded motivation's transient nature. He understood that self-care isn't merely a motivational endeavor but an obligation he owes to his mind and body.

This shift in perspective was a vital step in his journey towards sustainable self-improvement and personal growth, proving that creating an obligation to oneself when the world says otherwise can be a game-changer.

The After Session:

As a clinician, I used to work with clients to keep them *motivated* about self-care. It worked for a while. They noticed changes in themselves, learned to practice mindfulness, and made progress. But eventually, their motivation would change. It would come and go intermittently or die out altogether. Life often impacts our motivation for self-care, and that's OK.

But should we be encouraging more than merely helping clients stay **motivated** *to improve? Shouldn't it be more than that – a steady* **obligation** *to ourselves?*

Motivation can be temporary, but obligation breeds steady accountability. When we're obligated or committed to others, we don't want to fail them. If we fail to follow through, we'll be embarrassed, shamed, or negatively impacted. *What if we found ways to obligate ourselves to ourselves?*

We can put productive, self-accountability measures in place. For example, if we have difficulty saving money, we can find a local bank without many branches, open an account, deposit a percentage of our income, cut all electronic or debit card forms of payments, and limit our access to the account. We can put up barriers so we don't spend money we should save.

If we have thoughts of self-harm, we can ask a friend, therapist, or family member to hold on to the object we use, making it just a little more difficult to default to the problematic way of dealing with stressors. Addressing these issues requires much more than motivation. It requires an obligation to ourselves. When we have it, we can act on it to improve ourselves.

Motivation can be fleeting. As humans, we will run out of energy, get tired, stressed, and forgetful. We aren't machines, and exhaustion is a part of our condition. The critical difference is what we set in place when that happens. It is our obligation to ourselves and the commitment we've made to self-improvement that will help us stay on track when our motivation fades.

Make the obligation to yourself.

ANCHORING SELF-CARE IN STEADFAST COMMITMENT

Shane's journey through therapy highlights a transition from relying solely on motivation to embracing a steadfast obligation to self-care. This change reflects the importance of sustainable personal growth, where the commitment to oneself transcends the highs and lows of daily motivation. The therapeutic shift from encouraging momentary motivation to fostering a durable sense of self-obligation made a necessary shift in our approach to mental health.

Reflecting on Shane's experience, it is clear that while motivation is an excellent catalyst for initiating change, the commitment to oneself – viewed as an obligation – anchors long-term adherence to these changes. This commitment protects against the inevitable ebb and flow of life's challenges, ensuring that self-care remains a priority even when external pressures are high.

As Shane learned to view self-care as a desirable activity and a non-negotiable responsibility to himself, he established a more reliable framework for managing his well-being. This shift from motivation to obligation enhanced his resilience and equipped him with the tools to prioritize his health, regardless of his immediate circumstances.

Therefore, the concept of self-obligation emerges not merely as a therapeutic technique but as a life principle that can guide us towards more fulfilling and balanced lives. By internalizing this principle, Shane and others like him are better prepared to navigate the complexities of life without sacrificing their health and happiness.

PRACTICE: **DISCOVERING THE POWER OF SELF-OBLIGATION**
REFLECTIVE DIALOGUE

DATE:

Reflect on the idea of obligation to self. Consider this concept as a deeper level of commitment to your personal well-being beyond the fleeting nature of motivation.

What does *obligation to self* mean to me, and is it different from self-motivation?

_____
_____
_____
_____
_____
_____

How can increasing a sense of obligation towards my own well-being impact my life and choices?

_____
_____
_____
_____
_____
_____

What obstacles might I encounter when increasing my practice of self-obligation? (How can I overcome this?)

_____
_____
_____
_____
_____
_____

WEEK 2

DISCOVERING THE POWER OF SELF-OBLIGATION
REFLECTIVE JOURNALING

DATE:

For this week, focus on identifying areas in your life where self-obligation can be effectively implemented. Set aside a few minutes at the end of each day to review your answers to these prompts:

Identify an area of your life *(e.g., physical health, mental well-being, financial stability)* **where you could benefit from implementing self-obligation.**

_____
_____
_____
_____
_____

Describe any steps or measures to enforce this self-obligation
(e.g., setting aside a certain amount for monthly saving or committing to a daily mindfulness practice).

_____
_____
_____
_____
_____
_____

Identify, with specificity, what can be done this week to execute the measures/enforcement ideas for self-obligation (big or small).

_____
_____
_____

WEEK 2

DISCOVERING THE POWER OF SELF-OBLIGATION
REFLECTIVE JOURNALING

DATE:

Allocate at least one hour at the end of this week to address these prompts.

Reflect on how these self-obligation measures made you feel. Did you notice any resistance, or did it bring a sense of empowerment?

___

Reflect on your overall experience with self-obligation. How did it compare to relying solely motivation?

___

CHAPTER 3

Hurt a Little

Kelli:

Kelli is a Latinx woman who has long lived by the mantra "no pain, no gain." The idea that hardship is essential for growth was deeply embedded in her identity, influenced by her experiences as a woman and a person of color. This belief drove her to embrace difficulties in the name of self-improvement, linking pain and struggle with nearly every facet of her life. Over time, she became so accustomed to the discomfort that she could no longer discern the utility, growth, or purpose of her struggles. The inability to distinguish led her into a dangerous trap where she began hurting herself emotionally and physically in ways that were not beneficial or conducive to her growth. The struggle had become so intertwined with her self-perception that she began to lose sight of her worth and autonomy.

In our therapeutic process, we had to dismantle this belief carefully. We needed to shift her perspective from accepting struggle as an integral part of life to recognizing that she can choose what she wants to endure for her betterment and, more importantly, for her emotional freedom and daily autonomy.

Our sessions often involved revisiting challenging moments from Kelli's past. This process put her outside her comfort zone; usually, her initial reaction was resistance. She'd deflect, change topics, or retreat into silence – all signs of subconscious self-protection. For most of us, it's hard going over what we did to ourselves. Still, sometimes, it's the best option to ensure we don't continue to put ourselves in emotionally or physically harmful states of being. For Kelli, it was tough because he began intentionally hurting her emotional and physical being, thinking that it would lead to progress. Still, instead, it led her to want to end it all. So, she now was voiding all pain at any cost, unsure if it would lead to her thinking of hurting herself or to the progress she initially set out for when starting this journey. Whenever this happened, I'd gently remind her: "**Some things are supposed to hurt.**"

Yes, as her therapist, my role was multifaceted. I can sometimes model temporary supportive roles; the primary purpose was to provide a safe space for her to feel, understand, and confront her pain. The goal was to help her strengthen her emotional resilience, just as muscles grow stronger through repeated cycles of exertion and healing.

Through this process, Kelli understood that pain, when experienced in a controlled, safe environment, wasn't a punishment but an essential aspect of growth. It allowed for introspection, healing, and growth, unlike the internalized oppression, societal beliefs, and traumas she had carried, which only inflicted more emotional and physical pain. It was ok to face something if she had an intended goal or outcome that was specific, beneficial, and intended just for her.

By consistently "working out" in therapy, Kelli gradually learned to share her pain, strengthening her emotional resilience. In doing so, she knew how to voice her pain in other spaces and identify what was emotionally and physically equitable for her. This journey was certainly not easy, but it was pivotal for Kelli's progress toward a healthier, happier, and more confident life, affirming that controlled, intentional struggle can lead to profound personal growth.

The After Session:

Sometimes, after a client shares a difficult experience in a session, I ask them to bring their feelings to the forefront of their minds. I ask them to replay the challenging moments and bring to the surface the emotions they felt during their experience—right there in my office.

This puts many people outside of their comfort zones. Many have an immediate *"no"* reaction, while others find ways around their feelings.

Whenever I see this, I respond: *"You know, at some point, this is supposed to hurt."* Which prompts a perplexed look. I explain that, yes, I am here to be a support, a role model, a friend, a confidant, a brother, a father, whatever they need to process these feelings and make the therapeutic process easier. But beyond these supportive roles, I am, first and foremost, the therapist.

I model support so my clients can practice, and the emotional exercises serve as reference points outside of therapy. I give them a safe space to feel, explore, confront, and attempt to understand what it all means —if they choose. Permitting ourselves to hurt in a controlled and safe environment opens us to the greatest insight, healing, and growth.

This is much different than internalizing oppression, social beliefs, or traumas that we carry – which sometimes push us to inflict emotional pain (through negative self-talk) or physical pain through all forms of self-harm, including allowing ourselves to be subject to harm from another. Allowing pain to show up in a safe environment is not punishment. At times, it's necessary for growth, much like a muscle that tears so it can grow back bigger and stronger.

Therapy is the weight room. Our experiences are the barbell. And the therapist is the spotter.

The same is true of our emotions. The more we explore and face our difficult experiences, the better we can respond with emotional intelligence, ask for what we need, and identify what is emotionally and physically equitable for us. Hurting a little – in a controlled and risk-free environment – is a practice. I ask clients to share their pain because it strengthens the muscles we all need in other spaces. Eventually, doing so will help us live happier, healthier, more confident lives. This ensures we have the strength to continually seek and create safe spaces for ourselves and others.

PAIN & GROWTH - THE JOURNEY OF HEALING

Kelli's journey of transformation began with understanding and facing her pain. By challenging the ingrained belief that pain is a sign of progress, she began redefining her relationship with discomfort. This change was not merely about alleviating pain but about distinguishing its **origins and purposes,** allowing her to embrace only those struggles that are genuinely transformative.

The notion that "some things are supposed to hurt" is a necessary reminder within the therapeutic context. It isn't about endorsing suffering but acknowledging that discomfort is sometimes inevitable and essential in the process of growth. This perspective is crucial, especially when dismantling deeply embedded beliefs and traumas that do not serve the individual's well-being.

Through the sessions, Kelli learned to distinguish between destructive pain and constructive discomfort. She understood that the former stems from outdated beliefs and unresolved traumas, while the latter is part of a purposeful process toward self-improvement and emotional resilience. By focusing on controlled, intentional struggles, she began to identify what was truly beneficial for her growth.

As a therapist, my role was to guide Kelli through these complexities, offering a safe space to explore and confront her pain without judgment. The therapeutic space, akin to a weight room, provided the environment for Kelli to "work out" her emotional challenges. I acted as a spotter – ensuring she did not carry the weight alone.

Kelli's journey highlights the importance of emotional intelligence and the ability to voice one's pain as tools for healing. The ability to share her pain and request equitable emotional and physical spaces marked a significant milestone in her journey toward a healthier, more liberated life.

PRACTICE: **UNDERSTANDING OUR PAIN**   DATE:
REFLECTIVE DIALOGUE

Reflect on experiences where you've allowed yourself to experience discomfort for personal growth. Contrast this with a situation where you've experienced pain due to social structures or systemic forms of oppression. In your reflections, consider:

What have I done to distinguish the painful experience I have gone through? (Emotional or physical pain conducive to growth, or what shouldn't be a part of the life I want to live)

___

How have I allowed myself to interpret these experiences regarding my identity, and does this align with my desired understanding of who I am? (What did I tell myself these experiences mean about me, and do I like that narrative?)

___

NOTES

DATE:

WEEK 3 — **UNDERSTANDING OUR PAIN** — DAY 1
REFLECTIVE JOURNALING

Spend this week journaling about your daily experiences of stress, discomfort, or pain. It could be a challenging conversation at work, a physical workout, a personal setback, or an encounter with bias or discrimination. For each experience, reflect on:

What was a difficult experience today?

_____
_____
_____
_____
_____

How did it feel in the moment? What were you immediate reactions/responses?

_____
_____
_____

Does this situation contribute to your growth, or does it result from external or oppressive factors?

_____
_____
_____

Should you view this as a fault of your own, or is it a circumstance to learn from or strategize around?
(Consider if this is something you unnecessarily judge yourself for or integrate into your sense of self.)

_____
_____
_____

WEEK 3 — **UNDERSTANDING OUR PAIN**
REFLECTIVE JOURNALING — DAY 2

Spend this week journaling about your daily experiences of stress, discomfort, or pain. It could be a challenging conversation at work, a physical workout, a personal setback, or an encounter with bias or discrimination. For each experience, reflect on:

What was a difficult experience today?

_____
_____
_____
_____
_____

How did it feel in the moment? What were you immediate reactions/responses?

_____
_____
_____
_____

Does this situation contribute to your growth, or does it result from external or oppressive factors?

_____
_____
_____

Should you view this as a fault of your own, or is it a circumstance to learn from or strategize around?
(Consider if this is something you unnecessarily judge yourself for or integrate into your sense of self.)

_____
_____
_____

WEEK 3   **UNDERSTANDING OUR PAIN**   DAY 3
REFLECTIVE JOURNALING

Spend this week journaling about your daily experiences of stress, discomfort, or pain. It could be a challenging conversation at work, a physical workout, a personal setback, or an encounter with bias or discrimination. For each experience, reflect on:

What was a difficult experience today?

___

How did it feel in the moment? What were you immediate reactions/responses?

___

Does this situation contribute to your growth, or does it result from external or oppressive factors?

___

Should you view this as a fault of your own, or is it a circumstance to learn from or strategize around?
(Consider if this is something you unnecessarily judge yourself for or integrate into your sense of self.)

___

WEEK 3   **UNDERSTANDING OUR PAIN**   DAY 4
REFLECTIVE JOURNALING

Spend this week journaling about your daily experiences of stress, discomfort, or pain. It could be a challenging conversation at work, a physical workout, a personal setback, or an encounter with bias or discrimination. For each experience, reflect on:

What was a difficult experience today?

_____
_____
_____
_____

How did it feel in the moment? What were you immediate reactions/responses?

_____
_____
_____

Does this situation contribute to your growth, or does it result from external or oppressive factors?

_____
_____

Should you view this as a fault of your own, or is it a circumstance to learn from or strategize around?

(Consider if this is something you unnecessarily judge yourself for or integrate into your sense of self.)

_____
_____

WEEK 3   **UNDERSTANDING OUR PAIN**   DAY 5
REFLECTIVE JOURNALING

Spend this week journaling about your daily experiences of stress, discomfort, or pain. It could be a challenging conversation at work, a physical workout, a personal setback, or an encounter with bias or discrimination. For each experience, reflect on:

What was a difficult experience today?

_____
_____
_____
_____
_____

How did it feel in the moment? What were you immediate reactions/responses?

_____
_____
_____

Does this situation contribute to your growth, or does it result from external or oppressive factors?

_____
_____
_____

Should you view this as a fault of your own, or is it a circumstance to learn from or strategize around?
(Consider if this is something you unnecessarily judge yourself for or integrate into your sense of self.)

_____
_____
_____

| WEEK 3 | **UNDERSTANDING OUR PAIN**
REFLECTIVE JOURNALING | DAY 6 |

Spend this week journaling about your daily experiences of stress, discomfort, or pain. It could be a challenging conversation at work, a physical workout, a personal setback, or an encounter with bias or discrimination. For each experience, reflect on:

What was a difficult experience today?

_____

_____

_____

_____

_____

How did it feel in the moment? What were you immediate reactions/responses?

_____

_____

_____

Does this situation contribute to your growth, or does it result from external or oppressive factors?

_____

_____

_____

Should you view this as a fault of your own, or is it a circumstance to learn from or strategize around?
(Consider if this is something you unnecessarily judge yourself for or integrate into your sense of self.)

_____

_____

_____

WEEK 3   **UNDERSTANDING OUR PAIN**   DAY 7
REFLECTIVE JOURNALING

Spend this week journaling about your daily experiences of stress, discomfort, or pain. It could be a challenging conversation at work, a physical workout, a personal setback, or an encounter with bias or discrimination. For each experience, reflect on:

What was a difficult experience today?

_____
_____
_____
_____
_____

How did it feel in the moment? What were you immediate reactions/responses?

_____
_____
_____
_____

Does this situation contribute to your growth, or does it result from external or oppressive factors?

_____
_____

Should you view this as a fault of your own, or is it a circumstance to learn from or strategize around?
(Consider if this is something you unnecessarily judge yourself for or integrate into your sense of self.)

_____
_____
_____

A MOMENT OF GRACE

DATE:

To wrap up this week, find things to thank yourself for. Different from gratitude, for this task completion, the presence of another person, etc. Take this time to write some kind words about yourself, thanking yourself for who you are, what you've done, and what you're currently doing to show care and concern for who you are.

Giving yourself grace is about treating yourself with kindness and understanding, especially during times of difficulty or when you make mistakes. It involves recognizing that you are human and allowing yourself the same compassion and forgiveness you might offer others. This concept is essential in managing stress, promoting self-acceptance, and fostering a healthy mental and emotional state.

CHAPTER 4

Therapists Are Like Shoes

Grace:

Grace is a trans woman in her mid-30s who works as a professor in a small community college. Despite her professional accomplishments, Grace carries a deep-seated sense of inadequacy, partly stemming from her cultural background and experiences as a Black trans woman in a predominantly white community. Her upbringing ingrained the belief that she should be grateful for any help or attention she receives and should not question authority or other professionals. Internalized beliefs have caused Grace to devalue her own feelings, needs, and perspectives in therapeutic settings.

Grace sought therapy to address her feelings of imposter syndrome, a struggle with identity, and a growing sense of disconnection from her cultural roots. Yet, she found it challenging to engage with therapists who didn't seem to understand her cultural background or experiences. The subtle microaggressions, the inability to understand her lived experiences, and the disregard for the intersectionality of her identity were all barriers to her healing journey. Most therapists reaffirmed Grace's understanding that she was experiencing *"imposter syndrome."* Still, they failed to help her understand that the spaces she found herself in were designed, with specificity, to exclude people like her systematically and socially. She could never really be an imposter because, however, she showed up, she would never be welcomed. There is no imposter when all we carry is ourselves.

I first met Grace when she came for a consultation. She expressed her apprehension about therapy in general and disclosed her past experiences. She had been reluctant to voice her concerns about previous therapists, fearing it would reflect poorly on her rather than on their biases and, or incompetence.

I reassured her that finding the right therapist is very similar to finding the right pair of shoes. The therapy process should be centered on her needs. The goal is not to adapt herself to the therapist but to find a good fit for her. A therapeutic relationship, like a pair of shoes, should provide comfort and support and facilitate a journey toward self-understanding and healing.

Acknowledging her concerns, we ensured the therapy process was attuned to her needs. This included incorporating culturally sensitive practices, considering the intersectionality of her identity in understanding her challenges and prioritizing open communication where she could express her concerns or dissatisfaction freely.

We also developed strategies for Grace to assert her needs in personal and professional settings while working on ego strengthening and self-esteem. The therapy space became a place for her to challenge her ingrained beliefs, learn that her voice matters, and assert her right to seek and demand culturally competent care.

Grace's therapeutic journey focused not only on confronting her feelings of inadequacy but also on learning to prioritize her needs and advocate for herself. It underscored how we might misinterpret the reactions of the world around us as indications of our own flaws. She was taught that, much like selecting the right pair of shoes, she had the freedom to choose what was most suitable for her, even in therapy.

The After Session:

Therapists are like shoes. We should wear them, especially when we're out in the elements or on a path with rocks, sharp objects, and who knows what else on the ground in front of us. If the shoe doesn't fit or isn't appropriate for the journey, we shouldn't go barefoot, so we try on a different pair.

The same should be said when finding a therapist. If you're not getting what you need or making the progress you expect, have the conversation, then determine to try something else. Know that therapy doesn't always have to come in a clinical setting, a protocol, or an office couch. It can be found on the basketball court, at family dinners, or brunch with friends. And although we might have a favorite pair of shoes, that pair might only be best for some journeys.

Some of us get stuck in old relationships that were beneficial, positive, and transformational for one time or experience and expect them to help us address new needs. This can be the case with family members or lifelong friends. But we might need something else for a new challenge. We should keep the dancing shoes for the dance floor and get some sturdy hiking boots for the new mountain we plan to climb.

The analogy of therapists being like shoes is particularly true for those with a license to practice, treat, or consult on matters of the mind. In these sacred spaces, you should expect nothing other than to ensure you have a shoe that fits, is comfortable, and is sturdy enough to set out on the journey you're about to take.

In finding your pair of shoes, it's essential to be honest and genuine and express your concerns. You're also well in your right to ask for recommendations for new therapists and guidance and support while actively searching for someone new.

We work for you. Even if that work includes finding a different provider who can help meet your needs. You don't have to take what is given when it doesn't serve you, especially if you're trying to achieve self-improvement, healing, and personal change.

You get to pick your shoes. This process is for you.

EMPOWERMENT IN EVERY STEP

Grace's journey reminds us of the importance of personal agency in the healing process. Her experience highlights a crucial lesson that is applicable not only to therapy but to every aspect of life: *the significance of finding the right fit*. Whether it's a therapist, a job, or a relationship, the courage to demand environments that respect and understand one's identity is fundamental to personal growth and fulfillment.

Grace's story is about ensuring a therapeutic alliance that is truly responsive to the individual's unique cultural, personal, and professional contexts. By actively seeking out and insisting on culturally competent care, Grace not only challenged her feelings of inadequacy but also moved toward empowerment. She learned that her value does not diminish because of the perceptions or structural biases of the spaces she occupies. Instead, she discovered the strength in her voice and the right to assert her place in any setting.

The narrative of Grace's therapy is a call to all individuals, especially those from marginalized communities, to recognize their worth and the validity of their experiences. Reflecting the idea that true healing and understanding come from environments where one is seen, heard, and supported. Grace's evolving journey of self-advocacy and empowerment reflects a broader message: just as we would choose the right pair of shoes, we must also select the spaces and relationships that best suit our journey through life.

PRACTICE | **VOICING OUR NEEDS** | DATE:
REFLECTIVE DIALOGUE

Reflect on moments where you may have gained from taking the time to express yourself.

When have I felt the most misunderstood by someone who was supposed to support me (like a therapist or a close confidant)? How did it affect my self-esteem and my willingness to share your feelings?

NOTES

DATE:

| WEEK 4 | **VOICING OUR NEEDS**
REFLECTIVE JOURNALING | DAY 1 |

This week, you will receive a different journal prompt each day to help you explore and strengthen your voice. This week-long journey will guide you through reflection and the practice of self-advocacy, supporting your path to self-understanding and healing.

When have I felt the most misunderstood by someone who was supposed to support me (like a therapist or a close confidant)? How did it affect my self-esteem and my willingness to share your feelings?

NOTES

DATE:

WEEK 4 — **VOICING OUR NEEDS** — DAY 2
REFLECTIVE JOURNALING

Jot down instances where you asserted your needs, no matter how minor. Reflect on how expressing your needs affected your interactions. Were you understood? How did it make you feel?

NOTES

DATE:

WEEK 4 — **VOICING OUR NEEDS** — DAY 3
REFLECTIVE JOURNALING

Describe your ideal *'therapy shoes.'* What qualities would they have? How would they support you differently from your past experiences? Use this metaphor to consider what you truly need in a supportive environment or support network.

NOTES

DATE:

WEEK 4 — **VOICING OUR NEEDS** — DAY 4
REFLECTIVE JOURNALING

Consider a time when you realized a relationship (therapeutic or personal) wasn't serving your best interests. How did you come to this realization? What steps did you take, or wish you had taken, to find a better fit?

NOTES

DATE:

WEEK 4   **VOICING OUR NEEDS**   DAY 5
REFLECTIVE JOURNALING

Reflect on non-traditional therapy sources and support in your life (like sports, community gatherings, or hobbies). How do these experiences contribute to your sense of well-being and personal growth?

NOTES

DATE:

WEEK 4 — **VOICING OUR NEEDS** — DAY 6
REFLECTIVE JOURNALING

Think about a recent interaction where you successfully advocated for yourself. What did you do differently this time? How has your approach to self-advocacy changed over time?

NOTES

DATE:

WEEK 4 — **VOICING OUR NEEDS** — DAY 7
REFLECTIVE JOURNALING

Reflect on the ways you've shown yourself compassion and understanding this week. How has treating yourself with kindness influenced your mood, your interactions with others, and your self-esteem?

NOTES

DATE:

Remember, this is a space for reflection, honesty, and self-compassion. Write freely, knowing that this is a process. Progress might sometimes feel slow. But every step you take towards changing your internal dialogue is a victory worth celebrating.

CHAPTER 5

Our Operating Systems, and Our Apps

Gabby:

Gabby, a 28-year-old marketing executive, arrived for her first session wanting to work on her automatic negative thoughts. Despite her remarkable accomplishments and an outwardly successful life, Gabby battled an internal dialogue of constant self-doubt and criticism. She shared that she often felt she was *"not good enough."* These feelings seeped into her relationships and work, causing distress and an overwhelming sense of dissatisfaction.

One of the first things we addressed was the influence of societal messages on her subconscious mind. Gabby, a woman of color in a predominantly white industry, had been subtly subjected to societal messages and images that downplayed her worth and capabilities. These messages found their way into her subconscious, feeding her automatic negative thoughts and skewing her perception of herself.

We likened her mind to a smartphone or computer.

The apps running on the device were her responses, behaviors, and physical and emotional capacity. They were what she would open and use to engage with and react to the world and the people in her life. The capacity of the apps is heavily dependent on the operating system. We identified that her operating system was currently running an *"I'm

Not Good Enough Operating System," which colored her interpretation of her experiences and interactions.

Our therapy sessions aimed to delete this harmful programming and replace it with a healthier one. We started by helping Gabby recognize her automatic negative thoughts and their origins, tracing them back to societal messages and internalized beliefs. This awareness was crucial in helping her realize that these thoughts weren't inherent truths but rather programmed responses to external influences and life experiences.

Next, we created and implemented a *"worthiness"* operating system, focusing on positive affirmations, self-compassion exercises, and cognitive restructuring techniques. We aimed to reframe Gabby's internal dialogue and to counteract the negative societal messages.

Gabby was encouraged to curate her environment to reinforce positive messaging to further support this process. She sought out diverse, inclusive media, surrounded herself with supportive and affirming individuals, and incorporated symbols of strength and success that resonated with her personal and cultural background into her living and workspaces.

Over time, Gabby started to notice a shift in her thought patterns. The automatic negative thoughts became less frequent and less influential, replaced by affirming thoughts rooted in her genuine self-belief and resilience. The process was challenging and required consistent effort. Still, Gabby was committed to the journey, understanding that reprogramming her subconscious was crucial to her overall well-being and satisfaction in life.

The After Session:

When challenging automatic thoughts, thinking of our mind as having an operating system (OS) is helpful. The operating system determines how we show up in the world, ready to interpret and respond to what comes our way. Our responses – how we use our thoughts, beliefs, emotions, and experiences to interpret the world around us –

are the apps. We can only run whatever apps are compatible with the operating system hosting them.

So, if we hold a conscious or subconscious belief, the OS will find relevant information, gather any associated evidence, and make what we are plugging in real, tangible, and evident.

I use this example in sessions with clients who feel negatively about themselves. They discuss their accomplishments and the exceptional things that define their identity. They openly discuss the positive attributes they give to the world, and then they discuss their bewilderment about feeling alone, incomplete, and insufficient.

They often need clarification about the dissonance between their accomplishments, capabilities, responses, and thoughts of themselves.

"If I know all these great things about myself, why am I pushing away my spouse?"

"Why am I so easily irritable and anxious around loved ones?"

"Why do I feel alone in a room full of family and friends?"

Here's what I often say: It's because you tell yourself you do not deserve the love they're trying to give you or the connection they're attempting to make.

If we think we're unlovable, we won't allow them to love us fully because we can't compute the information they are giving or they can't see the true person we really are. So they end up loving the modified version instead of our authentic self—thus making it feel like we have no love at all. The mind makes the belief true; the program remains operable.

It's possible that every time a safe space is created for us, negative beliefs will disrupt the connection, or we won't allow ourselves to express what is needed for emotional safety. We withdraw and distance ourselves as the only adaptable means of protection.

The operating system is working but does not run the *"Authenticity"* program; it runs the *"I'm Not Deserving, There is Something Wrong With Me"* one.

What happens if we delete the bad programming and upload a healthier one? What if we run the *"Worthiness"* program that tells us we deserve and can be loved? The system is built to run whatever we feed it. So, while it might not be easy to make that switch, let's be mindful of the program we were running and know we have the power to change it.

EMBRACING THE WORTHINESS OPERATING SYSTEM

Gabby's therapy sessions focused on transitioning the *"I'm Not Good Enough"* operating system to a *"Worthiness"* operating system. The change in her internal dialogue showcases the power of mental and emotional reprogramming – a process for anyone dealing with automatic negative thoughts shaped by societal messages and internalized misconceptions.

Our work emphasized the importance of recognizing and addressing the roots of these thoughts. Gabby's courage to delve into the origins of her self-doubt has allowed her to dismantle the detrimental programming that once dictated her self-perception and interactions. By actively choosing to shift her mental framework, Gabby began to experience the world through a lens of self-compassion and authenticity.

This serves as a reminder that our mental operating system can be reconfigured. The narrative we carry about ourselves is not fixed or static; it is malleable and subject to revision through intentional action and guidance. Gabby showed me that the transformation to a healthier, affirming self-view is not just possible but is a journey worth undertaking.

Whether therapists or individuals are on their path to self-discovery, remember that the operating system of our mind sets the stage for every interaction and every personal reflection. When we upgrade to a system based on worthiness and self-acceptance, we not only enhance our own lives but also enrich the lives of those around us.

In embracing our worth, we allow ourselves to engage with life, unshackled by negative self-belief fully. Gabby's story is a testament to the resilience of the human spirit and the transformative power of love for self.

PRACTICE: **UNDERSTANDING OUR AUTOMATIC THOUGHTS** DATE:
REFLECTIVE DIALOGUE

Reflect on your personal journey towards replacing "I'm Not Good Enough" with the "Worthiness" program. Consider the following questions:

What societal messages or experiences have contributed to my automatic negative thoughts?

_____
_____
_____
_____
_____

How do these thoughts impact my relationships, work, and well-being?

_____
_____
_____
_____
_____
_____

How has becoming aware of these thought patterns influenced my view of myself and my interactions with others?

_____
_____
_____
_____
_____

PRACTICE: **UNDERSTANDING OUR AUTOMATIC THOUGHTS**
DATE:
REFLECTIVE DIALOGUE

Reflect on your personal journey towards replacing "I'm Not Good Enough" with the "Worthiness" program. Consider the following questions:

What steps can I take to curate my environment to support positive thought patterns?

_____
_____
_____
_____
_____

When was there a time when I noticed a shift in my thought pattern from negative to positive? How did it make me feel, and how did it impact the situation?

_____
_____
_____
_____
_____
_____
_____

Moving forward, what strategies can you use to continue feeding from prior experiences to switch from negative to positive thinking?

_____
_____
_____
_____
_____
_____

WEEK 5

UNDERSTANDING OUR AUTOMATIC THOUGHTS
REFLECTIVE DIALOGUE

DAY 1

Mindful Observation of Thought Patterns: Spend 3-5 minutes today in a quiet space, observing your thoughts as they arise. Try not to judge or engage with these thoughts. Instead, view them as if they are passing clouds in the sky. Identify any negative thoughts that may have come up and write down the emotions or situations that may trigger these regularly.

_____
_____
_____
_____
_____

Cognitive Restructuring Exercise: Write these automatic negative thoughts, if any, then challenge them. For each negative thought, write down a counteracting positive thought or affirmation. Practice saying these positive affirmations out loud.

NEGATIVE THOUGHT	COUNTERACTING THOUGHT
_____	_____
_____	_____
_____	_____
_____	_____
_____	_____
_____	_____
_____	_____

Write down this prompt and complete the sentence in the space provided below: "YOUR NAME" I love you today because...

_____
_____

WEEK 5

UNDERSTANDING OUR AUTOMATIC THOUGHTS
REFLECTIVE DIALOGUE

DAY 2

Mindful Observation of Thought Patterns: Spend 3-5 minutes today in a quiet space, observing your thoughts as they arise. Try not to judge or engage with these thoughts. Instead, view them as if they are passing clouds in the sky. Identify any negative thoughts that may have come up and write down the emotions or situations that may trigger these regularly.

_____
_____
_____
_____
_____
_____

Cognitive Restructuring Exercise: Write these automatic negative thoughts, if any, then challenge them. For each negative thought, write down a counteracting positive thought or affirmation. Practice saying these positive affirmations out loud.

NEGATIVE THOUGHT	COUNTERACTING THOUGHT
_____	_____
_____	_____
_____	_____
_____	_____
_____	_____
_____	_____

Write down this prompt and complete the sentence in the space provided below: "YOUR NAME" I love you today because...

_____
_____

WEEK 5

UNDERSTANDING OUR AUTOMATIC THOUGHTS
REFLECTIVE DIALOGUE

DAY 3

Mindful Observation of Thought Patterns: Spend 3-5 minutes today in a quiet space, observing your thoughts as they arise. Try not to judge or engage with these thoughts. Instead, view them as if they are passing clouds in the sky. Identify any negative thoughts that may have come up and write down the emotions or situations that may trigger these regularly.

_____
_____
_____
_____
_____

Cognitive Restructuring Exercise: Write these automatic negative thoughts, if any, then challenge them. For each negative thought, write down a counteracting positive thought or affirmation. Practice saying these positive affirmations out loud.

NEGATIVE THOUGHT	COUNTERACTING THOUGHT

Write down this prompt and complete the sentence in the space provided below: "YOUR NAME" I love you today because...

_____
_____

WEEK 5

UNDERSTANDING OUR AUTOMATIC THOUGHTS
REFLECTIVE DIALOGUE

DAY 4

Mindful Observation of Thought Patterns: Spend 3-5 minutes today in a quiet space, observing your thoughts as they arise. Try not to judge or engage with these thoughts. Instead, view them as if they are passing clouds in the sky. Identify any negative thoughts that may have come up and write down the emotions or situations that may trigger these regularly.

_____
_____
_____
_____
_____
_____

Cognitive Restructuring Exercise: Write these automatic negative thoughts, if any, then challenge them. For each negative thought, write down a counteracting positive thought or affirmation. Practice saying these positive affirmations out loud.

NEGATIVE THOUGHT	COUNTERACTING THOUGHT
_____	_____
_____	_____
_____	_____
_____	_____
_____	_____
_____	_____

Write down this prompt and complete the sentence in the space provided below: "YOUR NAME" I love you today because...

WEEK 5   **UNDERSTANDING OUR AUTOMATIC THOUGHTS**   **DAY 5**
REFLECTIVE DIALOGUE

Mindful Observation of Thought Patterns: Spend 3-5 minutes today in a quiet space, observing your thoughts as they arise. Try not to judge or engage with these thoughts. Instead, view them as if they are passing clouds in the sky. Identify any negative thoughts that may have come up and write down the emotions or situations that may trigger these regularly.

_____
_____
_____
_____
_____

Cognitive Restructuring Exercise: Write these automatic negative thoughts, if any, then challenge them. For each negative thought, write down a counteracting positive thought or affirmation. Practice saying these positive affirmations out loud.

NEGATIVE THOUGHT	**COUNTERACTING THOUGHT**
_____	_____
_____	_____
_____	_____
_____	_____
_____	_____
_____	_____
_____	_____

Write down this prompt and complete the sentence in the space provided below: "YOUR NAME" I love you today because...

_____
_____

WEEK 5

UNDERSTANDING OUR AUTOMATIC THOUGHTS
REFLECTIVE DIALOGUE

DAY 6

Mindful Observation of Thought Patterns: Spend 3-5 minutes today in a quiet space, observing your thoughts as they arise. Try not to judge or engage with these thoughts. Instead, view them as if they are passing clouds in the sky. Identify any negative thoughts that may have come up and write down the emotions or situations that may trigger these regularly.

_____
_____
_____
_____
_____

Cognitive Restructuring Exercise: Write these automatic negative thoughts, if any, then challenge them. For each negative thought, write down a counteracting positive thought or affirmation. Practice saying these positive affirmations out loud.

NEGATIVE THOUGHT	**COUNTERACTING THOUGHT**
_____	_____
_____	_____
_____	_____
_____	_____
_____	_____
_____	_____
_____	_____

Write down this prompt and complete the sentence in the space provided below: "YOUR NAME" I love you today because...

_____
_____

WEEK 5

UNDERSTANDING OUR AUTOMATIC THOUGHTS
REFLECTIVE DIALOGUE

DAY 7

Mindful Observation of Thought Patterns: Spend 3-5 minutes today in a quiet space, observing your thoughts as they arise. Try not to judge or engage with these thoughts. Instead, view them as if they are passing clouds in the sky. Identify any negative thoughts that may have come up and write down the emotions or situations that may trigger these regularly.

_____
_____
_____
_____
_____

Cognitive Restructuring Exercise: Write these automatic negative thoughts, if any, then challenge them. For each negative thought, write down a counteracting positive thought or affirmation. Practice saying these positive affirmations out loud.

NEGATIVE THOUGHT	COUNTERACTING THOUGHT

Write down this prompt and complete the sentence in the space provided below: "YOUR NAME" I love you today because...

_____
_____

ENVIRONMENTAL AUDIT:

DATE:

Look around your personal and work environments. Identify any objects, images, or even people that may be contributing to negative thought patterns. How can you replace or reframe these influences to support positive messaging and self-talk?

Remember, the purpose of these reflections is not to judge yourself but to foster self-understanding and personal growth. Be honest with yourself, but also be kind.

Self-exploration is a courageous act of vulnerability in itself.

CHAPTER 6

Acknowledge Your Feelings, Before It's Too Late.

Ethan:

Ethan, a 30-year-old, found his way to therapy because he felt numb and detached from his emotions.

Women he tried dating regularly told Ethan he seemed emotionally unavailable. Professionally successful and outwardly composed, Ethan, beneath the façade, was grappling with societal norms that perpetuated the notion of irrefutable strength, stoicism, and emotional fortitude, particularly among Black men. His internal turmoil was heightened by intergenerational trauma, societal expectations around masculinity, and the internalized oppression that had seeped into his daily life.

In our therapy sessions, Ethan described a childhood where emotional expression was regarded as a sign of weakness. Men were expected to be strong and silent, and any vulnerability was deemed a liability. This formed an emotional landscape where his feelings were not only disregarded but were also unsafe to express, which led him to develop a protective layer of *emotional numbness.*

We discussed his past, exploring instances where his emotional needs were dismissed or ridiculed, further instilling the damaging belief that he was not entitled to his emotions. His family, though well-meaning and supportive in many ways, unknowingly contributed to the stifling of his emotional expression – they were principally concerned with their own survival and overcoming their struggles. They sought to raise strong children who wouldn't allow the world to have the upper hand, but instead of discussing how the world's expectations may be problematic, they deemed the child's responses to be the issue. Unfortunately, some parents only know how to teach their children to "*fight through and never let 'em see them sweat.*"

Trying to balance *protection* and *preparation* can be complicated for a parent. This common theme plays out in many households, which is a product of generations of systemic oppression and racial trauma.

We discussed the discrepancy between logic and emotions. Ethan was suppressing his emotions because he couldn't logically explain them and feared being invalidated. His suppressed feelings had turned into an emotional time bomb waiting to explode.

As part of our therapy work, we challenged these internalized messages. I assigned Ethan to acknowledge his feelings in a journal, regardless of their size or perceived significance, to reconnect him with his emotional self. He was also encouraged to contemplate his reluctance to ask for emotional support, identify potential barriers, and slowly attempt to ask for what he needed emotionally from those around him.

We aimed to help Ethan understand that, despite what his upbringing and society had taught him, he was entitled to his full range of emotions and the accompanying human experience. We explored the possibility of vulnerability, showing him that it is a strength, not a weakness and that asking for support and comfort does not diminish his worth or masculinity.

Ethan's journey is ongoing and challenging. Yet, he is committed to breaking free from the chains of systemic factors and internalized beliefs that have kept him from accessing and expressing his emotions. By reclaiming his right to be vulnerable, feel, and ask for mitigation, he is reshaping his narrative and slowly changing how he presents himself to the world.

The After Session:

Like all human beings, Black men have an inherent right to experience the full spectrum of human emotions and experiences. These include strength, resilience, ambition, vulnerability, sensitivity, and emotionality – the observable behavioral and physiological components of emotion. Expressing a full emotional range is part of the human condition, allowing us to deeply connect with ourselves and others, cultivating empathy and understanding. Far too often, some are not allowed to be human, even in their own communities.

However, societal norms, stereotypes, and historical traumas have often created a rigid narrative around Black masculinity, suggesting that Black men must constantly embody strength, toughness, and stoicism. This expectation, pervasive and damaging, discourages Black men from expressing vulnerability and creates a cultural barrier to emotional health and well-being.

The concept of vulnerability is often misunderstood. It is not about being weak or submissive. Instead, it is about being open to experiences, emotions, and connections that can challenge us.

Vulnerability involves the courage to confront our feelings openly, whether they are feelings of love, fear, sadness, or joy.

By suppressing vulnerability, an integral aspect of emotional life, we can find ourselves at a disconnection, both from our internal emotional world and our relationships. This disconnection can lead to feelings of isolation, anxiety, and depression. It can also inhibit personal growth and self-understanding, preventing individuals from fully experiencing or learning from situations that evoke strong emotional responses.

There are several reasons why embracing vulnerability can be beneficial:

- **Improves Mental Health**: Acknowledging, expressing, and managing feelings are vital to maintaining good mental health. When we understand our emotions, we can better cope with stress, maintain more positive relationships, and make better decisions.
- **Fosters Deep Connections**: Being open and emotionally available allows us to connect with others on a deeper level. It can enhance relationships and open the door to mutual understanding and empathy.
- **Promotes Personal Growth**: We can often grow and learn by allowing ourselves to be vulnerable. Vulnerability can lead to greater self-knowledge, resilience, and personal development.
- **Challenges Stereotypes**: Embracing vulnerability challenges the harmful stereotype of the perpetually strong, invulnerable Black man, allowing for a more diverse and truthful representation of Black masculinity.
- **Empowers Others**: When Black men embrace their vulnerability, they not only liberate themselves but also model for other men – particularly young Black boys – that it's okay to express emotions, seek help, and be vulnerable.

Ultimately, Black men have as much a right as anyone else to explore the full range of this human experience. Acknowledging and embracing vulnerability, they affirm their humanity, complexity, and individuality. Encouraging this shift is vital in creating a society where everyone, including Black men, feels safe to be themselves in all their emotional complexity.

FULL SPECTRUM OF HUMANITY

As I reflect on Ethan's journey through therapy, it becomes evident that the challenges he faced are not just personal but are deeply rooted in the broader social and cultural contexts that shape our understanding of masculinity, particularly Black masculinity. Ethan's story shows the profound impact that societal norms and stereotypes have on the emotional lives of individuals, especially Black men, who are often compelled to navigate a constrained emotional landscape.

The narrative around Black masculinity, reinforced by historical trauma and societal expectations, has long dictated a limited role characterized by stoicism and strength. This restrictive narrative not only marginalizes the emotional experiences of Black men but also perpetuates a culture where expressions of vulnerability are seen as deviations rather than inherent aspects of the human condition. Ethan's therapeutic journey underscores the importance of challenging these internalized beliefs and societal norms, advocating for a holistic view of masculinity that includes vulnerability as a form of strength and an integral part of the emotional experience.

In therapy, Ethan learned to dismantle the walls he had built around his emotions, confronting the vulnerability he had long avoided. This process was not only about personal growth; it was about reclaiming his right to a whole emotional life, challenging the stereotypes that have historically oppressed Black men emotionally. His willingness to engage with his emotions and embrace vulnerability not only enhanced his own mental health and personal relationships but also served as a powerful counter-narrative to the stereotypes about Black masculinity.

The shift towards embracing vulnerability is crucial for cultivating deeper connections, enhancing mental health, and promoting personal growth. It also plays a vital role in challenging the harmful stereotypes that restrict the emotional expressions of Black men. By documenting and reflecting upon Ethan's experiences, I am able to advocate for a broader shift that acknowledges and supports the emotional diversity and humanity of Black men. This shift is essential for creating a society that values and upholds the emotional well-being of every individual, allowing them to experience the full spectrum of human emotions without fear of judgment or alienation.

PRACTICE: **THE POWER OF VULNERABILITY**
REFLECTIVE DIALOGUE

DATE:

Explore the theme of *"The Power of Vulnerability."* Use the following prompts to guide your inner dialogue

When have I felt the most vulnerable?

_____
_____
_____
_____
_____
_____

How did I feel during this moment of vulnerability?

_____
_____
_____
_____
_____
_____

Did I experience negative consequences as a result of my vulnerability (real or perceived)?

_____
_____
_____
_____
_____
_____

PRACTICE: **THE POWER OF VULNERABILITY**
REFLECTIVE DIALOGUE

DATE:

Explore the theme of *"The Power of Vulnerability."* Use the following prompts to guide your inner dialogue

What do I think the societal expectations of my masculinity/femininity are due to the experiences in my life?

___

How, if any, have these influenced my ability or willingness to express my emotions?

___

What fears or concerns do I have about showing vulnerability?

___

PRACTICE: **THE POWER OF VULNERABILITY**
REFLECTIVE DIALOGUE

DATE:

Explore the theme of *"The Power of Vulnerability."* Use the following prompts to guide your inner dialogue:

Why do I think these fears exist, and how can I address them?

_____
_____
_____
_____
_____

How would my life be different if I fully embraced my right to the full range of human emotion?

_____
_____
_____
_____
_____

How can I make space in my life to allow for emotional authenticity?

_____
_____
_____
_____
_____

PRACTICE: **THE POWER OF VULNERABILITY**
REFLECTIVE DIALOGUE

DATE:

Explore the theme of *"The Power of Vulnerability."* Use the following prompts to guide your inner dialogue:

When thinking of the role models in my life, did they show emotional vulnerability?

_____

How has their example influenced my thoughts on emotional expression?

_____

Write a quick *"thank you"* note to yourself for getting through these questions.

_____

WEEK 6 — **THE POWER OF VULNERABILITY** — DAY 1
REFLECTIVE JOURNALING

This week's journal exercise investigates your relationship with vulnerability and emotional expression. Spend some time (5-10 min) jotting down the emotions you felt today and how you responded to them.

Were there emotions that were easy to acknowledge and express today?

_____
_____

Were there emotions that were difficult to acknowledge or show today?

_____
_____
_____

Why were these emotions more challenging for you to express? Is it because of societal expectations, past experiences, or fears of judgment?

_____
_____
_____

Does the resistance to expressing these emotions affect your well-being, relationships, and perception of yourself?

_____
_____
_____

Are there possible benefits to being vulnerable to these emotions? How might your life change if you let yourself be more open with your emotions? What might be the potential positive outcomes?

_____
_____

WEEK 6 — **THE POWER OF VULNERABILITY** — **DAY 2**
REFLECTIVE JOURNALING

This week's journal exercise investigates your relationship with vulnerability and emotional expression. Spend some time (5-10 min) jotting down the emotions you felt today and how you responded to them.

Were there emotions that were easy to acknowledge and express today?

_____
_____

Were there emotions that were difficult to acknowledge or show today?

_____
_____
_____

Why were these emotions more challenging for you to express? Is it because of societal expectations, past experiences, or fears of judgment?

_____
_____
_____

Does the resistance to expressing these emotions affect your well-being, relationships, and perception of yourself?

_____
_____
_____

Are there possible benefits to being vulnerable to these emotions? How might your life change if you let yourself be more open with your emotions? What might be the potential positive outcomes?

_____
_____

WEEK 6   **THE POWER OF VULNERABILITY**   DAY 3
REFLECTIVE JOURNALING

This week's journal exercise investigates your relationship with vulnerability and emotional expression. Spend some time (5-10 min) jotting down the emotions you felt today and how you responded to them.

Were there emotions that were easy to acknowledge and express today?

_____

_____

Were there emotions that were difficult to acknowledge or show today?

_____

_____

_____

Why were these emotions more challenging for you to express? Is it because of societal expectations, past experiences, or fears of judgment?

_____

_____

_____

Does the resistance to expressing these emotions affect your well-being, relationships, and perception of yourself?

_____

_____

_____

Are there possible benefits to being vulnerable to these emotions? How might your life change if you let yourself be more open with your emotions? What might be the potential positive outcomes?

_____

_____

WEEK 6   **THE POWER OF VULNERABILITY**   DAY 4
REFLECTIVE JOURNALING

This week's journal exercise investigates your relationship with vulnerability and emotional expression. Spend some time (5-10 min) jotting down the emotions you felt today and how you responded to them.

Were there emotions that were easy to acknowledge and express today?

_____

_____

Were there emotions that were difficult to acknowledge or show today?

_____

_____

_____

Why were these emotions more challenging for you to express? Is it because of societal expectations, past experiences, or fears of judgment?

_____

_____

_____

Does the resistance to expressing these emotions affect your well-being, relationships, and perception of yourself?

_____

_____

_____

Are there possible benefits to being vulnerable to these emotions? How might your life change if you let yourself be more open with your emotions? What might be the potential positive outcomes?

_____

_____

WEEK 6 — **THE POWER OF VULNERABILITY** — DAY 5
REFLECTIVE JOURNALING

This week's journal exercise investigates your relationship with vulnerability and emotional expression. Spend some time (5-10 min) jotting down the emotions you felt today and how you responded to them.

Were there emotions that were easy to acknowledge and express today?

_____

_____

Were there emotions that were difficult to acknowledge or show today?

_____

_____

_____

Why were these emotions more challenging for you to express? Is it because of societal expectations, past experiences, or fears of judgment?

_____

_____

_____

Does the resistance to expressing these emotions affect your well-being, relationships, and perception of yourself?

_____

_____

_____

Are there possible benefits to being vulnerable to these emotions? How might your life change if you let yourself be more open with your emotions? What might be the potential positive outcomes?

_____

_____

WEEK 6   **THE POWER OF VULNERABILITY**   DAY 6
REFLECTIVE JOURNALING

This week's journal exercise investigates your relationship with vulnerability and emotional expression. Spend some time (5-10 min) jotting down the emotions you felt today and how you responded to them.

Were there emotions that were easy to acknowledge and express today?

_____

_____

Were there emotions that were difficult to acknowledge or show today?

_____

_____

_____

Why were these emotions more challenging for you to express? Is it because of societal expectations, past experiences, or fears of judgment?

_____

_____

_____

Does the resistance to expressing these emotions affect your well-being, relationships, and perception of yourself?

_____

_____

_____

Are there possible benefits to being vulnerable to these emotions? How might your life change if you let yourself be more open with your emotions? What might be the potential positive outcomes?

_____

_____

WEEK 6   **THE POWER OF VULNERABILITY**   DAY 7
REFLECTIVE JOURNALING

Use this outline to guide the process of embracing vulnerability in a structured and safe manner. Develop a plan for safely incorporating more vulnerability into your life. This could be small steps such as sharing a concern with a trusted friend or loved one, expressing an emotion you usually keep hidden or seeking professional help to explore your emotional landscape.

Define Vulnerability: Briefly describe what being vulnerable means to you.

_____
_____
_____

Identify Areas for Growth: List aspects of your life where you could be more open (emotions, fears, desires).

_____
_____
_____

Set Specific Goals: List small, manageable actions to increase vulnerability (sharing a personal story or expressing a hidden emotion).

_____
_____
_____
_____

Choose Safe Spaces and People: Identify people (trusted friends, family members) and environments (support groups, therapy, social functions) where you feel secure being vulnerable.

_____
_____

WEEK 6   **THE POWER OF VULNERABILITY**   DAY 7
REFLECTIVE JOURNALING

Plan Your Approach: Decide how you will start conversations or situations to share more openly (starting with less sensitive topics).

_____
_____
_____
_____
_____

Support Mechanisms: Consider ways to comfort yourself if responses aren't as expected (self-care activities or debriefing with a therapist). List aspects of your life where you could be more open (emotions, fears, desires).

_____
_____
_____
_____
_____
_____

Review and Reflect: Make a commitment to revisit your experiences with vulnerability, assessing what felt rewarding and what could be improved.

_____
_____
_____
_____
_____

CHAPTER 7

Self-Attunement

Robyn:

Robyn is a 42-year-old living in Washington, D.C. A devoted wife and mother of three, she embodies the caretaker role, always prioritizing her family's needs over her own. Robyn is a deeply respected member of the Chinese community and is known for her unwavering dedication to those around her. Her life has been characterized by her devotion to serving, loving, and providing for her family, so much so that she has lost sight of her needs and desires. Despite the bustling family life that surrounds her, she often feels alone and empty.

Robyn has come to therapy to understand these feelings of loneliness and emptiness and to learn how to better care for herself. In our initial sessions, I asked Robyn to describe her daily routine. It quickly became apparent that her days were filled with activities catered to her family's needs. Whether preparing meals, helping with schoolwork, or coordinating family activities, Robyn was constantly in service of others.

Robyn described a constant state of exhaustion, but it was clear it wasn't just physical exhaustion but emotional. She was pouring everything she had into everyone around her while neglecting her needs and emotions in the process.

We began to work on the concept of self-attunement.

This involved helping Robyn understand the importance of being aware of her own emotional presence, just as she was mindful of those around her.

We discussed the need to respect and respond to her own emotions the same way she respected and responded to those of her loved ones. Initially, Robyn was resistant, citing cultural expectations and her chosen role as a wife and mother. We explored these beliefs and how they were impacting her well-being. Over time, Robyn began to see that by ignoring her own needs, she was undermining her ability to care for her family in the way she wanted.

We practiced boundaries and wellness exercises to help Robyn tune into her physical and emotional states. We also discussed strategies for self-care and making time for her own interests and needs. Slowly, Robyn began to understand the value of caring for herself and became more comfortable acknowledging and expressing her feelings. We focused on learning to attune to her own needs and emotions, just as she does for those she loves. Although challenging, Robyn has begun to see that by caring for herself, she's improving not only her own well-being but also the overall happiness and health of her family.

The After Session:

Attunement, generally speaking, is awareness of another's emotional presence.

We become attuned when we sense them, create a rhythm, or share an affect. This experience is likened to "sharing the same skin" or reaching a more profound sense of empathy and commonality. Attunement is often needed to create lasting bonds between two people. When we're attuned, *you feel what I feel*. We're connected, and we can't be undone unless we choose to break our bond.

Now imagine, for a moment, if we applied this to ourselves – looking inward. What if we responded to our own feelings the same way we honored and responded to the emotions of others we care about? We must yearn to find attunement with ourselves. We must strive for an unbreakable relationship with *"the self"* where we acknowledge and attune to what our mind and body need, even when we can't make sense of it.

Our feelings can create physiological responses in the body. Neglecting them can lead to anxiety, depression, irritability, isolation, you name it. Self-attunement is about correcting our views and changing our tendencies to internalize, overanalyze, or consciously disregard our feelings. It's about aligning our emotions, understanding ourselves, and forming a bond with the inner self to survive what life throws at us.

Self-attunement involves constantly checking in and asking what the mind and body need. It's OK to attune to ourselves just as we attune to others – giving ourselves the same care and concern we give others and giving ourselves the positive self-talk and assurances we offer to them.

Establishing a relationship with our inner self makes it easier to pour in self-love, positive regard, self-understanding, and personal acceptance. We'll learn to love ourselves once we condition ourselves to be just as responsive to our needs as we are to the needs of others.

SELF-ATTUNEMENT—A JOURNEY TO INNER HARMONY

Robyn has allowed us to witness her transformation from a state of self-neglect to one of self-attunement. As I reflect on her experiences, the significance of this transformation extends beyond her individual story to resonate with a universal truth: the necessity of nurturing our own emotional and physical well-being in order to truly care for others.

Robyn's initial resistance to self-care, rooted in cultural norms and personal expectations, highlights a common barrier many face in prioritizing their own needs. The cultural expectation that she must always be a giver, constantly attuned to the needs of her family, had led her to a state of emotional depletion. However, through therapy, Robyn has begun to recognize that self-attunement is not a deviant act of selfishness but rather a fundamental aspect of sustaining our capacity to give.

The sessions highlighted the transformative power of recognizing and responding to our own emotional state. Just as Robyn had mastered the art of tuning into the needs of her family, she learned to apply these skills inwardly, fostering a nurturing relationship with herself. This shift not only alleviated her feelings of loneliness and emptiness but also improved her interactions with her loved ones, making her care more sustainable and joy-filled.

As Robyn continues to embrace self-attunement, she serves as an example to others who may struggle with similar challenges. Her journey is a reminder that true attunement begins within and that by honoring our own emotions and needs, we lay the foundation for more authentic and enduring connections to others.

PRACTICE: **SELF-ATTUNEMENT**
REFLECTIVE DIALOGUE
DATE:

Take a few minutes to answer these questions focused on self-attunement.

What barriers do I have in remaining connected to my emotional and physical needs?

___

What is the difference between the person I am for the world and my inner self, and what makes me feel freer?

___

What fears inhibit me from connecting to myself or honoring what I feel when I feel it?

___

Do I know who I am, and if I'm unsure, who do I want to be?

___

PRACTICE: **SELF-ATTUNEMENT**
REFLECTIVE DIALOGUE
DATE:

This week, adjust your journal practice by integrating 5-10 minutes of meditation or mindfulness focused on self-attunement (preferably in the morning).

Find a quiet place, take deep breaths, and allow yourself to feel present in the moment. Try to identify any emotions you are feeling and understand why you are feeling this way. Remember, this isn't about analyzing or judging your feelings but acknowledging and accepting them as they are. Then, think of one activity you could do today for yourself. This can bring you a moment of reprieve, gratitude, joy, or peace—a short walk, reading a book, or even a quiet cup of tea. This activity should make you feel like you are being good to yourself just because you can. Not collateral to anyone, anything, or task. Commit

How and at what time of the day will I take 5-10 minutes for myself this week?

_____
_____
_____
_____
_____

Are there any barriers to this, and if so, who do I need to collaborate with to ensure I can, or can hold me accountable?

_____
_____
_____
_____
_____

What excuses do I usually make that stop me from doing something that might be good for me?

_____
_____

Remember, this is a journey, and taking small steps is okay. The goal is not perfection but increasing self-awareness and self-attunement.

WEEK 7   **SELF-ATTUNEMENT**   DAY 1
REFLECTIVE JOURNALING

This week, adjust your journal practice by integrating 5-10 minutes of meditation or mindfulness focused on self-attunement-examining your feelings at the moment (preferably in the morning).

Answer the first three questions first, then complete question four at the end of the day.

1. What emotions did you notice during this practice?

___

___

___

2. What will you do today to increase/maintain this emotion (if positive)

___

___

___

3. What will you do today to change this emotion if you need to create a better feeling?

___

___

___

4. If you could take time for yourself today, write how it felt and write a quick thank-you note to yourself. If you couldn't take time today, write what you learned may be a barrier, and you'll try to change moving forward.

___

___

WEEK 7 | **SELF-ATTUNEMENT** | DAY 2
REFLECTIVE JOURNALING

This week, adjust your journal practice by integrating 5-10 minutes of meditation or mindfulness focused on self-attunement-examining your feelings at the moment (preferably in the morning).

Answer the first three questions first, then complete question four at the end of the day.

1. What emotions did you notice during this practice?

_____
_____
_____

2. What will you do today to increase/maintain this emotion (if positive)

_____
_____
_____

3. What will you do today to change this emotion if you need to create a better feeling?

_____
_____
_____

4. If you could take time for yourself today, write how it felt and write a quick thank-you note to yourself. If you couldn't take time today, write what you learned may be a barrier, and you'll try to change moving forward.

_____
_____

WEEK 7 **SELF-ATTUNEMENT** DAY 3
REFLECTIVE JOURNALING

This week, adjust your journal practice by integrating 5-10 minutes of meditation or mindfulness focused on self-attunement-examining your feelings at the moment (preferably in the morning).

Answer the first three questions first, then complete question four at the end of the day.

1. What emotions did you notice during this practice?

_____

_____

_____

2. What will you do today to increase/maintain this emotion (if positive)

_____

_____

_____

3. What will you do today to change this emotion if you need to create a better feeling?

_____

_____

_____

4. If you could take time for yourself today, write how it felt and write a quick thank-you note to yourself. If you couldn't take time today, write what you learned may be a barrier, and you'll try to change moving forward.

_____

_____

WEEK 7 | **SELF-ATTUNEMENT** | DAY 4
REFLECTIVE JOURNALING

This week, adjust your journal practice by integrating 5-10 minutes of meditation or mindfulness focused on self-attunement-examining your feelings at the moment (preferably in the morning).

Answer the first three questions first, then complete question four at the end of the day.

1. What emotions did you notice during this practice?

_____
_____
_____

2. What will you do today to increase/maintain this emotion (if positive)

_____
_____
_____

3. What will you do today to change this emotion if you need to create a better feeling?

_____
_____
_____

4. If you could take time for yourself today, write how it felt and write a quick thank-you note to yourself. If you couldn't take time today, write what you learned may be a barrier, and you'll try to change moving forward.

_____
_____

| WEEK 7 | **SELF-ATTUNEMENT** | DAY 5 |

REFLECTIVE JOURNALING

This week, adjust your journal practice by integrating 5-10 minutes of meditation or mindfulness focused on self-attunement-examining your feelings at the moment (preferably in the morning).

Answer the first three questions first, then complete question four at the end of the day.

1. What emotions did you notice during this practice?

_____

_____

_____

2. What will you do today to increase/maintain this emotion (if positive)

_____

_____

_____

3. What will you do today to change this emotion if you need to create a better feeling?

_____

_____

_____

4. If you could take time for yourself today, write how it felt and write a quick thank-you note to yourself. If you couldn't take time today, write what you learned may be a barrier, and you'll try to change moving forward.

_____

_____

WEEK 7 — **SELF-ATTUNEMENT** — DAY 6
REFLECTIVE JOURNALING

This week, adjust your journal practice by integrating 5-10 minutes of meditation or mindfulness focused on self-attunement-examining your feelings at the moment (preferably in the morning).

Answer the first three questions first, then complete question four at the end of the day.

1. What emotions did you notice during this practice?

_____
_____
_____

2. What will you do today to increase/maintain this emotion (if positive)

_____
_____
_____

3. What will you do today to change this emotion if you need to create a better feeling?

_____
_____
_____

4. If you could take time for yourself today, write how it felt and write a quick thank-you note to yourself. If you couldn't take time today, write what you learned may be a barrier, and you'll try to change moving forward.

_____
_____

WEEK 7 — **SELF-ATTUNEMENT**
REFLECTIVE JOURNALING — DAY 7

This week, adjust your journal practice by integrating 5-10 minutes of meditation or mindfulness focused on self-attunement-examining your feelings at the moment (preferably in the morning).

Answer the first three questions first, then complete question four at the end of the day.

1. What emotions did you notice during this practice?

___

2. What will you do today to increase/maintain this emotion (if positive)

___

3. What will you do today to change this emotion if you need to create a better feeling?

___

4. If you could take time for yourself today, write how it felt and write a quick thank-you note to yourself. If you couldn't take time today, write what you learned may be a barrier, and you'll try to change moving forward.

___

WEEK 7 — **SELF-ATTUNEMENT** — DAY 7
REFLECTIVE JOURNALING

Review your entries. Try to identify any patterns or trends in your feelings and emotional states. Also, consider how your self-care activity has affected your daily routine and interactions with your family. How has it changed your perspective on taking care of your own needs? Write a reflection on these observations and any changes you want to implement going forward.

_____
_____
_____
_____
_____
_____
_____
_____
_____
_____
_____
_____
_____
_____
_____
_____
_____
_____
_____
_____
_____
_____
_____
_____

NOTES

DATE:

CHAPTER 8

Self-Love = Revolution

Amber:

Amber grew up to be everything she knew she would be. She had many examples of what *not* to be through her parents' and siblings' mistakes and the world's view, which included the expected place for her. She was also very aware of what would happen if she stepped out of these expected norms.

Early on, Amber was responsible for her siblings and remained accountable for everyone in the family, including her parents. Although many around her are proud of her accomplishments and have a physical presence in her life, she still feels incredibly lonely and empty. Amber had always known that her place was based on what everyone needed – her utility to others.

Due to her socioeconomic status growing up, she believed she was never desirable or worthy of being poured into, so she poured into everyone else. Internalized oppression and sexism were deeply rooted in Amber's understanding of herself and her place in the world. She believed she had to settle for relationships that didn't serve her and for being treated in ways inconsistent with the love she deserved.

Amber arrived at my office, physically and emotionally drained week after week, burdened by the demands of being a woman of color at a law firm and by the expectations of those in her life who consistently treated her as an afterthought.

During one of our sessions, she became visibly upset. I had encouraged her to express something she was reluctant to share. As a person, not just a clinician, it was difficult for me to watch her deteriorate over time without ever receiving or allowing herself to receive. I asked Amber if she believed she deserved to receive as much as she gave and whether she should keep making room for those who only take from her.

Continuing to make room in her life – both emotionally and physically – for those unwilling or unable to meet her needs does not support the belief that she deserves more. She immediately thought I was blaming her for her current situation, and maybe I was in a way, but it took some work to help her understand that the way you allow people to show up in your life is how they will continue to show up. We set the standard, and everyone else around follows suit.

In another session, I asked her, "What is the biggest barrier to loving yourself more?" Her response: *"I haven't poured into myself enough to know what the barriers are, or if they exist at all."* She sat in silence, coming to the realization that she needed to work on the concept of loving herself.

What do we do to show our mind and body that we have care and concern for them?

From childhood, Amber experienced things that led her to believe they were the standard ways to treat her body, and she accepted certain things told to her that took root in her mind. If sexual trauma or emotional abuse were her baseline of existence in the world, how could I expect her to come up with a different understanding of her mind and body? This was the thought she expressed, looking back at me in the silence of our session.

She was reconciling the concept that she needed to learn to love herself. This was the first and primary step to ensuring that there would always be love around her. Treating herself like someone who mattered, someone who was cared for and, dare we say, **loved**, was a brand new concept. We would spend the subsequent sessions planning strategically for this. Spending as much thought and intention on herself as she did on others was more than new. It was revolutionary.

The After Session:

revolutionary
/ˌrevəˈlo͞oSHəˌnerē/
adjective
1. Involving or causing a complete or dramatic **change**.

In today's world, actively participating in self-love is revolutionary.

It can be a revolutionary act for a person to get out of bed, put on clothes, carve out time for a commute during the workday, travel to her therapist's office, sit on the couch, and participate in something that she knows will make her feel better.

We are rarely encouraged to love ourselves. Even rarer are voices encouraging us to love ourselves just for the sake of it – or the health of it – without some perceived "*need*" for self-improvement.

We seldom hear, "*This body and mind have value.*"

Loving yourself can be a revolutionary act. Why? Because it goes against everything society says someone should think about themselves. So, when clients come to my office for the first time, I walk them over to an open space with a collection of books, sound bowls, yoga mats, meditation devices, and other electronic or manual tools for self-care. I explain that the space is for practicing what we discuss in therapy. It is theirs to use before, after, or whenever the office is open. Nine times out of ten, people say, "*I won't need that.*" That's because, for most of society, self-care and self-love are reserved for specific people – those who need "*fixing,*" are broken, or don't like who they are. There must be a *reason* why someone needs five minutes to practice self-care. They must be compensating for something...

Of course, this could not be further from the truth. As I said in the session, we all need "something to send the body and the mind the message that you love them both." We don't need any reason to practice self-love other than wanting to and exploring our power to improve our attitudes about ourselves. We can exercise this power regularly, daily, however, and whenever we choose. We can practice even if we are already happy with ourselves. Why not double down on another dose of self-love?

Society has brainwashed us to believe that giving to ourselves in an emotionally and physically positive way is a bad thing. We've internalized this, and it's tainted the concept of caring for the mind and the body. People often say we come into the world grieving. At birth, we mourn the comfort of our mother's womb – the safety, warmth, and security. We enter a world that is noisy and individualistic, which, right at the start, dumps all the preconceived notions of who we are supposed to be based on our skin color, sex, or ethnic makeup.

That is the world we grow up in – a world where we have to be this and can't be that. We can't be too Black, too bold, too strong, too confident, too weak, too bright, too woke, too emotional, or too **FREE**.

We must stay within society's accepted lines.

It's still far too rare for a child to be told, "It's okay to love who you are exactly as you are." Yet repeating this affirmation throughout life is essential. It's often easier to change things about ourselves if we love them. The motivation for change is self-love, not fitting into a box, conforming to a standard, or trying to eliminate an unlovable part of ourselves. Positive change and growth can also come from loving the things we tell ourselves we want to change. We rarely hear people say we're perfectly imperfect and that if we want to, we can choose to keep perfecting our perfection.

What do we have to lose by loving ourselves a little more? Caring about ourselves doesn't have to be attached to anything. We can choose to care simply because we can.

So, I challenge you: Be revolutionary.

THE REVOLUTIONARY ACT OF SELF-LOVE

Amber is another example of the transformative power of self-love and internal reflection. Her story is not just her own but echoes the silent battles we all face in a world that often dictates who people should be rather than embracing who they are. Through her sessions, we witnessed a profound metamorphosis – from a life of serving others to understanding the paramount importance of serving oneself.

Amber's transition into acknowledging and accepting self-love as a revolutionary act brings to light the broader societal challenges and internalized norms that frequently sideline personal well-being. Her bravery in confronting these norms and challenging the status quo of self-neglect underscores a crucial narrative: self-care and self-love are not acts of rebellion against societal expectations but are essential for genuine well-being.

Amber's journey serves as an open invitation for all to reflect on their own self-love practices. It challenges each of us to recognize the revolutionary act of prioritizing our mental and emotional health. The simple yet profound act of loving ourselves is both a personal victory and a radical shift in how we interact with the world around us.

PRACTICE — **EMBRACING SELF-COMPASSION & LOVE**   DATE:
REFLECTIVE DIALOGUE

Consider the concept of self-compassion. This process involves embracing your unique self, understanding that you are entitled to want what you want, and offering yourself the compassion you would extend to a friend or family member.

How can I practice giving myself permission, grace, and acceptance of my desires, actions, and feelings?

_____
_____
_____
_____
_____

How might a shift in my self-perception impact my life and your well-being?

_____
_____
_____
_____
_____
_____

Write a quick note to yourself providing this compassion, outlining your thoughts, and thanking yourself for who you are.

_____
_____
_____
_____
_____

EMBRACING SELF-COMPASSION & LOVE — DAY 1
REFLECTIVE DIALOGUE

For this exercise, focus on showing up authentically in the world with clear intentions for each day. Start by setting an intention each morning, which will guide you throughout the day, whether you practice mindfulness, prioritize self-care, or speak up for yourself. At the end of the day, reflect and journal about your experiences.

EX: Today, I intend to find peace in small or passing moments / **Today, I will show up in the world as** someone who honors what they are feeling without judgment

Today, I intend to _____

_____

Today, I will show up in the world as someone who _____

_____

1. What was your intention for the day, and how did it guide your actions?

_____

_____

2. Can you identify any instances where you acted in alignment with your intention?

_____

_____

3. What happened today that required you to give yourself grace and understanding?

_____

_____

4. How did this practice of setting an intention and reflecting on it affect your overall day?

_____

_____

WEEK 8   **EMBRACING SELF-COMPASSION & LOVE**   DAY 2
REFLECTIVE DIALOGUE

For this exercise, focus on showing up authentically in the world with clear intentions for each day. Start by setting an intention each morning, which will guide you throughout the day, whether you practice mindfulness, prioritize self-care, or speak up for yourself. At the end of the day, reflect and journal about your experiences.

EX: Today, I intend to find peace in small or passing moments / **Today, I will show up in the world as** someone who honors what they are feeling without judgment

Today, I intend to _____
_____

Today, I will show up in the world as someone who _____
_____

1. What was your intention for the day, and how did it guide your actions?
_____
_____

2. Can you identify any instances where you acted in alignment with your intention?
_____
_____

3. What happened today that required you to give yourself grace and understanding?
_____
_____

4. How did this practice of setting an intention and reflecting on it affect your overall day?
_____
_____

WEEK 8   **EMBRACING SELF-COMPASSION & LOVE**   DAY 3
REFLECTIVE DIALOGUE

For this exercise, focus on showing up authentically in the world with clear intentions for each day. Start by setting an intention each morning, which will guide you throughout the day, whether you practice mindfulness, prioritize self-care, or speak up for yourself. At the end of the day, reflect and journal about your experiences.

EX: Today, I intend to find peace in small or passing moments / **Today, I will show up in the world as** someone who honors what they are feeling without judgment

Today, I intend to _____
_____

Today, I will show up in the world as someone who _____
_____

1. What was your intention for the day, and how did it guide your actions?
_____
_____

2. Can you identify any instances where you acted in alignment with your intention?
_____
_____

3. What happened today that required you to give yourself grace and understanding?
_____
_____

4. How did this practice of setting an intention and reflecting on it affect your overall day?
_____
_____

WEEK 8   **EMBRACING SELF-COMPASSION & LOVE**   DAY 4
REFLECTIVE DIALOGUE

For this exercise, focus on showing up authentically in the world with clear intentions for each day. Start by setting an intention each morning, which will guide you throughout the day, whether you practice mindfulness, prioritize self-care, or speak up for yourself. At the end of the day, reflect and journal about your experiences.

EX: Today, I intend to find peace in small or passing moments / **Today, I will show up in the world as** someone who honors what they are feeling without judgment

Today, I intend to _____

_____

Today, I will show up in the world as someone who _____

_____

1. What was your intention for the day, and how did it guide your actions?

_____

_____

2. Can you identify any instances where you acted in alignment with your intention?

_____

_____

3. What happened today that required you to give yourself grace and understanding?

_____

_____

4. How did this practice of setting an intention and reflecting on it affect your overall day?

_____

_____

WEEK 8 — **EMBRACING SELF-COMPASSION & LOVE** — DAY 5
REFLECTIVE DIALOGUE

For this exercise, focus on showing up authentically in the world with clear intentions for each day. Start by setting an intention each morning, which will guide you throughout the day, whether you practice mindfulness, prioritize self-care, or speak up for yourself. At the end of the day, reflect and journal about your experiences.

EX: Today, I intend to find peace in small or passing moments / **Today, I will show up in the world as** someone who honors what they are feeling without judgment

Today, I intend to _____

_____

Today, I will show up in the world as someone who _____

_____

1. What was your intention for the day, and how did it guide your actions?

_____

_____

2. Can you identify any instances where you acted in alignment with your intention?

_____

_____

3. What happened today that required you to give yourself grace and understanding?

_____

_____

4. How did this practice of setting an intention and reflecting on it affect your overall day?

_____

_____

EMBRACING SELF-COMPASSION & LOVE
REFLECTIVE DIALOGUE

WEEK 8 — **DAY 6**

For this exercise, focus on showing up authentically in the world with clear intentions for each day. Start by setting an intention each morning, which will guide you throughout the day, whether you practice mindfulness, prioritize self-care, or speak up for yourself. At the end of the day, reflect and journal about your experiences.

EX: **Today, I intend** to find peace in small or passing moments / **Today, I will show up in the world as** someone who honors what they are feeling without judgment

Today, I intend to _____

_____

Today, I will show up in the world as someone who _____

_____

1. What was your intention for the day, and how did it guide your actions?

_____

_____

2. Can you identify any instances where you acted in alignment with your intention?

_____

_____

3. What happened today that required you to give yourself grace and understanding?

_____

_____

4. How did this practice of setting an intention and reflecting on it affect your overall day?

_____

_____

WEEK 8   **EMBRACING SELF-COMPASSION & LOVE**   DAY 7
REFLECTIVE DIALOGUE

For this exercise, focus on showing up authentically in the world with clear intentions for each day. Start by setting an intention each morning, which will guide you throughout the day, whether you practice mindfulness, prioritize self-care, or speak up for yourself. At the end of the day, reflect and journal about your experiences.

EX: **Today, I intend** to find peace in small or passing moments / **Today, I will show up in the world as** someone who honors what they are feeling without judgment

Today, I intend to _____

_____

Today, I will show up in the world as someone who _____

_____

1. What was your intention for the day, and how did it guide your actions?

_____

_____

2. Can you identify any instances where you acted in alignment with your intention?

_____

_____

3. What happened today that required you to give yourself grace and understanding?

_____

_____

4. How did this practice of setting an intention and reflecting on it affect your overall day?

_____

_____

CHAPTER 9

Shifting Worlds

Liam:

Working with Liam as a therapist has been a deeply emotional experience.

Liam was first brought to my office by his mother, who noticed a growing rage and irritability within him. She was concerned by the constant fights and the outbursts he seemed to have at school. As I started working with Liam, the complexity of his situation soon unfolded before me.

His world was one where he had to be constantly alert and always ready to adjust his behavior based on the spaces he found himself in. As a young boy navigating an environment that viewed him as a threat, his interactions were vastly different based on the color of his backpack or the positioning of his hands. He was continuously navigating being "too dangerous," "too loud," "too unkempt," or "too expressive."

The consequences of these adjustments were severe, leading him to respond with anger and rage. Whether it was changing his schedule to avoid uncomfortable interactions with a woman in his building or feigning ignorance in school to avoid being seen as 'too intelligent,' Liam's daily life was a series of forced concessions. Each decision, far from being made freely, was a strategic move to navigate an acceptable existence in the eyes of others. These accommodations, though seemingly minor and appropriate at first, were taking a significant toll on his mental and emotional health. The only place where he could be himself, free from the constant need to adjust, was his room at home. When this sanctuary was invaded, eruptions of uncontrollable rage ensued.

Each day, his autonomy was chipped away. His sense of self-control waned with each interaction, which required him to adjust his behavior and identity. It seemed as if the only control he had left was during those brief ten minutes on Thursday afternoons when he was home alone.

His mother had brought him to me with an expectation for a diagnosis, perhaps believing that a professional therapeutic opinion could explain her son's responses and rationalize her and the school's concerns. However, as I sat across from Liam, hearing his experiences, I realized that the solution wasn't about pathologizing his experiences. Instead, it was about validating them – showing Liam that he had a right to his space, time, and identity without needing adjustment. My role as a therapist became not to diagnose but to empower. My goal was to let Liam know his experiences were valid and his emotions justified.

The anger and rage he was feeling were not symptoms of an underlying pathology but rather a natural response to being forced into a constant state of adjustment. Together, we began to work on strategies to help him assert his boundaries and claim spaces where he could express his true self without the fear of judgment, harm to his body or emotions, or the need to adjust. In his healing journey, the goal is to manage anger and rage and redefine the narrative. The new narrative is that existing freely doesn't mean being a threat and that Liam has the right to exist without constantly adjusting himself to suit the expectations of others.

Working with Liam, I was reminded that the role of a therapist is not just to help facilitate the healing process but also to advocate and be a voice for those like Liam who are continually fighting against systems that may need to adjust for them.

The After Session:

What message do we send when we constantly adjust for others, and at what point do we determine that it's the world's turn to adjust for us?

We often find ourselves trying to find comfort in spaces that aren't built or intended for us. Each time we accommodate someone else, we tell ourselves a message of worth, value, or necessity. We honor the environment, dynamic, or response from others over those messages when we allow ourselves to adjust to everyone around us.

It's one thing to choose to shift our way of being for those we choose to love: a parent, child, or life partner. We accommodate and make space for others, and this is necessary. But finding the balance and preserving space for ourselves is just as important. It's possible to occupy a space that isn't detrimental to our way of being and to accommodate others when the accommodation doesn't cause us physical, emotional, or mental anguish.

So, the question remains: how much should we adjust? There is a profound strength in knowing when to bend and when to stand firm, recognizing that while compromise is part of human interaction, *self-erasure* is not. We must strive for a world where our adaptations are choices that enhance our lives rather than diminish them.

Ultimately, we all have a choice in how we interact with the world around us. By recognizing the value of standing our ground when necessary, we create growth opportunities for ourselves and those around us. In this dance of give and take, remember that it's okay to pause, reflect, and ask if the adjustments are mutual, beneficial, or detrimental to how we view and treat ourselves.

Perhaps it's time for a shift in dynamics, where instead of constantly molding ourselves to fit the spaces we enter, we push back and start shaping those spaces to fit us better.

EMBRACING AUTONOMY IN ADJUSTMENT

Through Liam's therapeutic journey, we've delved deep into the intricacies of a young boy's struggle to maintain his identity in a world that relentlessly asks him to change. From navigating his environment with a heightened sense of vigilance to the eruptions of rage stemming from the invasion of his private refuges, Liam's journey is a reminder of the psychological toll of continuous adaptation.

As I reflect, the question of how much one should adjust lingers. It encapsulates the essence of our interactions with the world and ourselves. The shift from adjustment for survival to adjustment for meaningful existence is not just a therapeutic goal but a societal imperative. Liam's experiences reflect the destructive consequences of a world that does not accommodate the unique dimensions of each individual.

The concept urges us to foster environments where individuals like Liam do not just survive but thrive. It challenges societal structures to evolve and accommodate diversity genuinely and equitably. As therapists, caregivers, parents, and community members, our role extends beyond the confines of therapy sessions. We are advocates for a world that embraces difference, values emotional health, and acknowledges the intrinsic worth of every individual without demanding constant concession.

PRACTICE — **"ADJUSTMENTS & BOUNDARIES"**
REFLECTIVE DIALOGUE

DATE:

This reflective exercise is designed to help you identify moments when you're adjusting too much for others. Hopefully, it will also allow you to envision a future where you can assert your needs and set healthier boundaries.

In what situations have I felt that I need to adjust who I am, my behavior, or compromise my needs for someone else?

_____
_____
_____
_____
_____
_____
_____
_____
_____

How did it make me feel, and what can I do differently to balance my own needs with those of others in the future?

_____
_____
_____
_____
_____
_____
_____

WEEK 9   **"ADJUSTMENTS & BOUNDARIES"**   DAY 1
REFLECTIVE JOURNALING

Spend some time each day this week writing about your daily interactions and experiences. Use the following questions to guide your reflections:

1. Identify moments of adjustment: Were there moments in your day where you felt you had to adjust yourself to accommodate someone else? Describe these moments in detail.

_____
_____
_____
_____
_____

2. Reflect on your feelings: How did these moments make you feel? Was there frustration, anxiety, resentment, or maybe relief in some cases?

_____
_____
_____
_____
_____

3. Potential alternatives: Imagine how the interaction could have gone differently if you asserted your needs and set boundaries. What would you have said or done differently?

_____
_____
_____
_____
_____

WEEK 9 — **"ADJUSTMENTS & BOUNDARIES"** — DAY 1
REFLECTIVE JOURNALING

Spend some time each day this week writing about your daily interactions and experiences. Use the following questions to guide your reflections:

4. Personal Impact: Reflect on how these constant adjustments affect your sense of self and your relationship with others. Are there patterns you notice?

_____
_____
_____
_____
_____
_____
_____
_____
_____
_____

5. Potential alternatives: Imagine how the interaction could have gone differently if you asserted your needs and set boundaries. What would you have said or done differently?

_____
_____
_____
_____
_____
_____

WEEK 9   **"ADJUSTMENTS & BOUNDARIES"**   DAY 2
REFLECTIVE JOURNALING

Spend some time each day this week writing about your daily interactions and experiences. Use the following questions to guide your reflections:

1. Identify moments of adjustment: Were there moments in your day where you felt you had to adjust yourself to accommodate someone else? Describe these moments in detail.

_____

_____

_____

_____

_____

_____

2. Reflect on your feelings: How did these moments make you feel? Was there frustration, anxiety, resentment, or maybe relief in some cases?

_____

_____

_____

_____

_____

_____

3. Potential alternatives: Imagine how the interaction could have gone differently if you asserted your needs and set boundaries. What would you have said or done differently?

_____

_____

_____

_____

_____

WEEK 9   **"ADJUSTMENTS & BOUNDARIES"**   **DAY 2**
REFLECTIVE JOURNALING

Spend some time each day this week writing about your daily interactions and experiences. Use the following questions to guide your reflections:

4. Personal Impact: Reflect on how these constant adjustments affect your sense of self and your relationship with others. Are there patterns you notice?

_____
_____
_____
_____
_____
_____
_____
_____
_____
_____
_____

5. Potential alternatives: Imagine how the interaction could have gone differently if you asserted your needs and set boundaries. What would you have said or done differently?

_____
_____
_____
_____
_____
_____

WEEK 9   **"ADJUSTMENTS & BOUNDARIES"**   DAY 3
REFLECTIVE JOURNALING

Spend some time each day this week writing about your daily interactions and experiences. Use the following questions to guide your reflections:

1. Identify moments of adjustment: Were there moments in your day where you felt you had to adjust yourself to accommodate someone else? Describe these moments in detail.

_____
_____
_____
_____
_____
_____

2. Reflect on your feelings: How did these moments make you feel? Was there frustration, anxiety, resentment, or maybe relief in some cases?

_____
_____
_____
_____
_____

3. Potential alternatives: Imagine how the interaction could have gone differently if you asserted your needs and set boundaries. What would you have said or done differently?

_____
_____
_____
_____
_____

WEEK 9　　　**"ADJUSTMENTS & BOUNDARIES"**　　　DAY 3
　　　　　　　　　REFLECTIVE JOURNALING

Spend some time each day this week writing about your daily interactions and experiences. Use the following questions to guide your reflections:

4. **Personal Impact:** Reflect on how these constant adjustments affect your sense of self and your relationship with others. Are there patterns you notice?

_____
_____
_____
_____
_____
_____
_____
_____
_____
_____

5. **Potential alternatives:** Imagine how the interaction could have gone differently if you asserted your needs and set boundaries. What would you have said or done differently?

_____
_____
_____
_____
_____
_____

WEEK 9   **"ADJUSTMENTS & BOUNDARIES"**   DAY 4
REFLECTIVE JOURNALING

Spend some time each day this week writing about your daily interactions and experiences. Use the following questions to guide your reflections:

1. Identify moments of adjustment: Were there moments in your day where you felt you had to adjust yourself to accommodate someone else? Describe these moments in detail.

___

2. Reflect on your feelings: How did these moments make you feel? Was there frustration, anxiety, resentment, or maybe relief in some cases?

___

3. Potential alternatives: Imagine how the interaction could have gone differently if you asserted your needs and set boundaries. What would you have said or done differently?

___

WEEK 9　　　**"ADJUSTMENTS & BOUNDARIES"**　　　DAY 4
REFLECTIVE JOURNALING

Spend some time each day this week writing about your daily interactions and experiences. Use the following questions to guide your reflections:

4. Personal Impact: Reflect on how these constant adjustments affect your sense of self and your relationship with others. Are there patterns you notice?

_____
_____
_____
_____
_____
_____
_____
_____
_____
_____

5. Potential alternatives: Imagine how the interaction could have gone differently if you asserted your needs and set boundaries. What would you have said or done differently?

_____
_____
_____
_____
_____

WEEK 9 — **"ADJUSTMENTS & BOUNDARIES"** — DAY 5
REFLECTIVE JOURNALING

Spend some time each day this week writing about your daily interactions and experiences. Use the following questions to guide your reflections:

1. Identify moments of adjustment: Were there moments in your day where you felt you had to adjust yourself to accommodate someone else? Describe these moments in detail.

_____
_____
_____
_____
_____

2. Reflect on your feelings: How did these moments make you feel? Was there frustration, anxiety, resentment, or maybe relief in some cases?

_____
_____
_____
_____
_____

3. Potential alternatives: Imagine how the interaction could have gone differently if you asserted your needs and set boundaries. What would you have said or done differently?

_____
_____
_____
_____
_____

WEEK 9   **"ADJUSTMENTS & BOUNDARIES"**   DAY 5
REFLECTIVE JOURNALING

Spend some time each day this week writing about your daily interactions and experiences. Use the following questions to guide your reflections:

4. Personal Impact: Reflect on how these constant adjustments affect your sense of self and your relationship with others. Are there patterns you notice?

_____
_____
_____
_____
_____
_____
_____
_____
_____
_____

5. Potential alternatives: Imagine how the interaction could have gone differently if you asserted your needs and set boundaries. What would you have said or done differently?

_____
_____
_____
_____
_____
_____

WEEK 9   **"ADJUSTMENTS & BOUNDARIES"**   DAY 6
REFLECTIVE JOURNALING

Spend some time each day this week writing about your daily interactions and experiences. Use the following questions to guide your reflections:

1. Identify moments of adjustment: Were there moments in your day where you felt you had to adjust yourself to accommodate someone else? Describe these moments in detail.

___

2. Reflect on your feelings: How did these moments make you feel? Was there frustration, anxiety, resentment, or maybe relief in some cases?

___

3. Potential alternatives: Imagine how the interaction could have gone differently if you asserted your needs and set boundaries. What would you have said or done differently?

___

WEEK 9 — **"ADJUSTMENTS & BOUNDARIES"** — DAY 6
REFLECTIVE JOURNALING

Spend some time each day this week writing about your daily interactions and experiences. Use the following questions to guide your reflections:

4. Personal Impact: Reflect on how these constant adjustments affect your sense of self and your relationship with others. Are there patterns you notice?

_____
_____
_____
_____
_____
_____
_____
_____
_____
_____
_____

5. Potential alternatives: Imagine how the interaction could have gone differently if you asserted your needs and set boundaries. What would you have said or done differently?

_____
_____
_____
_____
_____
_____

WEEK 9   **"ADJUSTMENTS & BOUNDARIES"**   DAY 7
REFLECTIVE JOURNALING

Spend some time each day this week writing about your daily interactions and experiences. Use the following questions to guide your reflections:

1. Identify moments of adjustment: Were there moments in your day where you felt you had to adjust yourself to accommodate someone else? Describe these moments in detail.

___

2. Reflect on your feelings: How did these moments make you feel? Was there frustration, anxiety, resentment, or maybe relief in some cases?

___

3. Potential alternatives: Imagine how the interaction could have gone differently if you asserted your needs and set boundaries. What would you have said or done differently?

___

WEEK 9	**"ADJUSTMENTS & BOUNDARIES"**	DAY 7
	REFLECTIVE JOURNALING	

Spend some time each day this week writing about your daily interactions and experiences. Use the following questions to guide your reflections:

4. Personal Impact: Reflect on how these constant adjustments affect your sense of self and your relationship with others. Are there patterns you notice?

_____
_____
_____
_____
_____
_____
_____
_____
_____
_____

5. Potential alternatives: Imagine how the interaction could have gone differently if you asserted your needs and set boundaries. What would you have said or done differently?

_____
_____
_____
_____
_____

Remember, change takes time, and it's okay to take small steps toward this goal. Celebrate the progress, however small, and be kind to yourself throughout this process.

CHAPTER 10

Freedom and Free Will

Carmen:

Carmen, approaching forty, is a single woman dedicated to social justice and caring for her aging mother. As her therapist, I saw a person grappling with societal pressures and internalized beliefs about *"singlehood"* and personal worth. Despite her successful career and the richness of her personal life, Carmen came to therapy with a heavy heart, burdened by the idea that her single status was a sign of failure, and was haunted by the question of what was *"wrong"* with her.

During our sessions, we explored the heavy mantle of responsibility Carmen carried. She felt that her life had been a series of adjustments to meet her mother's needs and societal expectations. We delved into her past relationships, unraveling the threads of her romantic life to understand why Cameron believed they hadn't worked out. She internalized a harsh script that measured her worth against her relationship status, and this narrative was reinforced by cultural norms and the subtle yet persistent messages she received as a woman in her community.

Carmen's therapy journey was about dismantling these narratives and uncovering the layers of her unconscious beliefs. We used Assata Shakur's vision of freedom as a guiding principle – the right to grow and blossom into whomever she is meant to be, regardless of her relationship status. Cameron began to understand that not every relationship was a failure but an evolution. She could have been married and *"freed"* from singlehood long ago. However, as she understood more about herself over time, she realized those relationships were for a different Cameron at a different stage. Moving forward and letting them go *was a success*. She was now freeing herself from what didn't serve her, both consciously and subconsciously, as she began to explore the depth of her emotions, the capacity to pour love into herself, and to see herself as she wanted to be seen, not as an imposed image of what others or society might expect of someone as beautiful and intelligent as she knew herself to be.

In addition to her relationship status, she often struggled with having the freedom to express her emotions, expectations, and brilliance. Even in her own community, Cameron sometimes felt the same constant demand to fight the angry woman stereotype just for correcting someone's error, providing a sensible suggestion, or leading a team with the highest quarterly returns of any department at her agency.

Our goal was to redefine what success, fulfillment, and freedom meant for Carmen, independent of the expectations imposed on her. Almost every choice she made was a habitual response aimed at distancing herself from the negative stereotypes she believed were associated with being single, intelligent, and financially independent. We worked toward recognizing her right to make choices that align with her desires and well-being. Through our sessions, Carmen understood that being single did not equate to being incomplete. She started to embrace her freedom, not just as the absence of a partner, but as the presence of choice, growth, and the blossoming of her true self. Carmen is learning to live freely, making decisions not out of habit or compulsion but from a place of self-love and authenticity. This led to her continued developing a relationship with herself and budding relationships with others.

The After Session:

"Freedom? You're asking me about freedom? I'll be honest with you. I know a whole lot more about what freedom isn't than about what it is,

because I've never been free... The way I see it, freedom is the right to grow, is the right to blossom. Freedom is the right to be yourself, to be who you are, to be who you wanna be, to do what you wanna do." - Assata Shakur.

Are we genuinely exercising free will when making impulsive decisions, seemingly unattached to anything or anyone? Does going with what *"feels good"* always equate to freedom? When are we totally free?

If the choices that bring the *"feel good"* or acceptance of what's *"right"* are rooted in current expectations and past experiences, then is the decision-making process one of free will or habit? When solving problems, responding, and reacting out of habit, are we allowing old scripts to interfere with our choices, creating a process where pain still affects us even though we are far removed from it?

For some, the habitual decision to abandon what makes us free is conditioned either by our upbringing or by negative interactions we've had with others because we don't fit the box in which we're expected to reside. If we continue to follow this, can we ever choose life freely? Can we be free if our decisions are seemingly not made freely?

In therapy, the client and therapist collectively try to get to the root and uncover the "unknowns" that might contribute to how we communicate, the people we're attracted to, and the impulsive, habitual decisions we tend to make. So, we go through our discovery process, evaluate family dynamics and traumatic or joyful experiences, and discover emotions our body remembers even when we have long forgotten. We dig to uncover the reasons behind how we treat ourselves and others – our learned behaviors.

What do we do next once we become aware of our unconscious thoughts and how they impact our behavior? Contrary to popular belief, healing does not automatically flow from tapping into the unconscious. For instance, just because we can become aware that our lack of a secure attachment in childhood causes us to long for love – but we still run when it comes – doesn't mean our loneliness will disappear. Consciously, we want to be loved, but our behavior sometimes doesn't match us. This cognitive dissonance can come from habit(s)-

conditioning. All the repeated experiences in our life that allowed the habit of choosing not to love freely.

Although we might like to think that possessing all the pieces of the puzzle makes us whole, this may not be the case. Understanding why we self-sabotage or hold negative beliefs about what we have – or lack – does not automatically resolve our issues. Why do we choose the wrong partners or react similarly in distressing situations? True wholeness might come from making choices not dictated by expectations, habits, or societal confines.

Connecting the conscious to the subconscious can provide further options. We've made the leap and are at the point where we can see all the good, the bad, the learned behaviors, and the habits picked up in our environments. We can now see what we might have been using for comfort or because it was the only thing available when we were at our lowest. When we see the best and the worst of ourselves, we understand the psychological, environmental, and biological factors affecting how we show up in the world and then act based on our understanding of these; this is when we're operating in freedom.

Even if we hold the mirror in front of us and know what each string does when pulled, we may still make the same old choices even after we've exposed all the things that make us who we are. Or we may choose otherwise. The only difference is that we now have options. And they have been created for us, by us. The option to go with what we know, with a complete understanding of why we've always made this choice, or the option to choose something else. These choices are no longer habitual or driven by the unknown. Choosing to stay the same or making a change once we know all the cards on the table might be our exact moment of free will. All that's left is to accept and love who we are, with the entire understanding of "me," or move toward who we want to be and what we want out of life.

Now, life is about choices, decisions, and making another choice based on what we've learned, what we feel, and what we want.

TRUE FREEDOM

As Carmen's therapeutic journey unfolded, I witnessed an awakening to the genuine essence of freedom – navigating the complex interplay of societal expectations, internalized narratives, and the relentless pursuit of personal authenticity. Carmen's journey reflects the struggle and the beauty of rediscovering oneself beyond the confines of predefined roles and stereotypes.

Throughout our sessions, Carmen gradually dismantled the shackles of "singlehood" as a measure of failure, redefining success and fulfillment on her own terms. Her evolution was not just about negating her past but also about embracing a future where her choices reflect her deepest desires and insights, rather than reacting to external pressures or past conditioning.

Carmen symbolizes the broader quest for freedom that many face—freedom from the labels society attaches to us, from the roles we are expected to play, and from the internalized scripts that dictate our self-worth. Her therapy was a voyage towards understanding that true freedom lies in the right to choose one's path without apology or justification, recognizing that every step taken is part of a larger, dynamic process of self-realization.

Carmen's freedom was beautifully encapsulated by Assata Shakur's reflections on growth and self-becoming. Carmen learned to live not by avoiding the old but by consciously choosing the new, equipped with an awareness of her own needs and desires, and the invaluable lessons gleaned from each experience. Her life's narrative shifts from a tale of seeking validation to one of celebrating the intrinsic worth and potential that was hers all along.

THE AFTER SESSION WORKBOOK — 153

PRACTICE

"THE CHOICE IS MINE"
REFLECTIVE JOURNALING

DATE:

This exercise is designed to help us practice freedom and free will daily. It's a week-long exercise focusing on making conscious choices that reinforce personal growth and self-empowerment.
Reflect on your growth and any patterns you noticed over the years.

Finish the sentence below:
As I have grown in years, I have also grown in the following ways:

_____
_____
_____
_____
_____
_____

What decisions can I regularly make that will lead to greater freedom?

_____
_____
_____
_____
_____
_____

What insights have I gained from my life experience?

_____
_____
_____
_____
_____

WEEK 10   **"THE CHOICE IS MINE"**   DATE:
REFLECTIVE JOURNALING

This week-long journaling exercise is designed to enhance personal growth and self-empowerment by practicing freedom and free will through daily conscious choices. Each day, dedicate 5-10 minutes in the morning to reflection and creating daily affirmations. In the evening, spend another 5-10 minutes reviewing your day's decisions, evaluating your choices, and reflecting on your experiences.

MORNING JOURNALING INSTRUCTIONS:

Reflections (1-5 minutes):
Start each day with a brief meditation or quiet reflection. Focus on what you hope to achieve or experience today—a feeling, an action, or an insight.

Daily Affirmations (1-5 minutes):
After reflecting, craft a set of personal affirmations that emphasize your independence and personal power.

Examples include *"I am the architect of my life," "I'm learning to make choices that are right for me,"* or *"I am learning to embrace my freedom to grow and blossom."*

EVENING JOURNALING INSTRUCTIONS:

Decision Points (throughout the day):
Identify at least three moments in your day when you make decisions automatically. These could involve routine choices like selecting a meal, deciding how to spend your lunch break, or how you respond to interactions with others. Note these moments where you might act on autopilot or against what you consciously want.

Deliberate Choices (1-2 minutes each):
At each identified decision point, pause and consider your options. Challenge your habitual response by asking, *"What do I truly want?"* Choose in a way that aligns with your genuine desires, whether the same as your usual choice or different—the key is to make a mindful decision.

Reflection(s) (5-10 minutes):
Conclude your day by reflecting on your choices. Consider the outcomes and any differences from your typical day. Consider how this practice of intentional decision-making has influenced your sense of autonomy and empowerment.

WEEK 10   **"THE CHOICE IS MINE"**   DAY 1
REFLECTIVE JOURNALING

Each day, allocate 5-10 minutes in the morning for reflection and creating daily affirmations, followed by another 5-10 minutes in the evening to review and evaluate your day's decisions and experiences.

MORNING JOURNALING

Reflection: What do you hope to experience or achiever today?

_____
_____
_____
_____
_____
_____
_____

TODAY'S AFFIRMATION(S)

_____	_____
_____	_____
_____	_____
_____	_____
_____	_____
_____	_____

Write down this prompt and complete the sentence in the space provided below: "YOUR NAME" I love you today because...

_____
_____

WEEK 10   **"THE CHOICE IS MINE"**   DAY 1
REFLECTIVE JOURNALING

Each day, allocate 5-10 minutes in the morning for reflection and creating daily affirmations, followed by another 5-10 minutes in the evening to review and evaluate your day's decisions and experiences.

EVENING JOURNALING

Decision Points (throughout the day): Identify at least three moments in the day you made decisions automatically.

_____
_____
_____
_____
_____

Deliberate Choices (1-2 minutes each): For each identified decision point, consider what options (if any) you may have.

_____
_____
_____
_____
_____

Reflection(s) (5-10 minutes): Conclude your day by reflecting on your choices, outcomes, desired changes, and what was intentional/unintentional.

_____
_____
_____
_____

WEEK 10 | **"THE CHOICE IS MINE"** | DAY 2
REFLECTIVE JOURNALING

Each day, allocate 5-10 minutes in the morning for reflection and creating daily affirmations, followed by another 5-10 minutes in the evening to review and evaluate your day's decisions and experiences.

MORNING JOURNALING

Reflection: What do you hope to experience or achiever today?

___

TODAY'S AFFIRMATION(S)

___

Write down this prompt and complete the sentence in the space provided below: "YOUR NAME" I love you today because...

___

WEEK 10   **"THE CHOICE IS MINE"**   **DAY 2**
REFLECTIVE JOURNALING

Each day, allocate 5-10 minutes in the morning for reflection and creating daily affirmations, followed by another 5-10 minutes in the evening to review and evaluate your day's decisions and experiences.

EVENING JOURNALING

Decision Points (throughout the day): Identify at least three moments in the day you made decisions automatically.

_____
_____
_____
_____
_____
_____

Deliberate Choices (1-2 minutes each): For each identified decision point, consider what options (if any) you may have.

_____
_____
_____
_____
_____
_____

Reflection(s) (5-10 minutes): Conclude your day by reflecting on your choices, outcomes, desired changes, and what was intentional/unintentional.

_____
_____
_____
_____
_____

THE AFTER SESSION WORKBOOK — 159

WEEK 10 + **"THE CHOICE IS MINE"** DAY 3
REFLECTIVE JOURNALING

Each day, allocate 5-10 minutes in the morning for reflection and creating daily affirmations, followed by another 5-10 minutes in the evening to review and evaluate your day's decisions and experiences.

MORNING JOURNALING

Reflection: What do you hope to experience or achiever today?

_____
_____
_____
_____
_____
_____
_____

TODAY'S AFFIRMATION(S)

_____   _____
_____   _____
_____   _____
_____   _____
_____   _____
_____   _____
_____   _____

Write down this prompt and complete the sentence in the space provided below: "YOUR NAME" I love you today because...

_____
_____
_____

WEEK 10 +   **"THE CHOICE IS MINE"**   **DAY 3**
REFLECTIVE JOURNALING

Each day, allocate 5-10 minutes in the morning for reflection and creating daily affirmations, followed by another 5-10 minutes in the evening to review and evaluate your day's decisions and experiences.

EVENING JOURNALING

Decision Points (throughout the day): Identify at least three moments in the day you made decisions automatically.

_____
_____
_____
_____
_____
_____

Deliberate Choices (1-2 minutes each): For each identified decision point, consider what options (if any) you may have.

_____
_____
_____
_____
_____
_____

Reflection(s) (5-10 minutes): Conclude your day by reflecting on your choices, outcomes, desired changes, and what was intentional/unintentional.

_____
_____
_____
_____

WEEK 10   **"THE CHOICE IS MINE"**   DAY 4
REFLECTIVE JOURNALING

Each day, allocate 5-10 minutes in the morning for reflection and creating daily affirmations, followed by another 5-10 minutes in the evening to review and evaluate your day's decisions and experiences.

MORNING JOURNALING

Reflection: What do you hope to experience or achiever today?

_____
_____
_____
_____
_____
_____
_____

TODAY'S AFFIRMATION(S)

Write down this prompt and complete the sentence in the space provided below: "YOUR NAME" I love you today because...

_____
_____
_____

WEEK 10   **"THE CHOICE IS MINE"**   DAY 4
REFLECTIVE JOURNALING

Each day, allocate 5-10 minutes in the morning for reflection and creating daily affirmations, followed by another 5-10 minutes in the evening to review and evaluate your day's decisions and experiences.

EVENING JOURNALING

Decision Points (throughout the day): Identify at least three moments in the day you made decisions automatically.

_____
_____
_____
_____
_____
_____

Deliberate Choices (1-2 minutes each): For each identified decision point, consider what options (if any) you may have.

_____
_____
_____
_____
_____
_____

Reflection(s) (5-10 minutes): Conclude your day by reflecting on your choices, outcomes, desired changes, and what was intentional/unintentional.

_____
_____
_____
_____
_____

WEEK 10 | **"THE CHOICE IS MINE"** | DAY 5
REFLECTIVE JOURNALING

Each day, allocate 5-10 minutes in the morning for reflection and creating daily affirmations, followed by another 5-10 minutes in the evening to review and evaluate your day's decisions and experiences.

MORNING JOURNALING

Reflection: What do you hope to experience or achiever today?

___

TODAY'S AFFIRMATION(S)

___

Write down this prompt and complete the sentence in the space provided below: "YOUR NAME" I love you today because...

WEEK 10   **"THE CHOICE IS MINE"**   **DAY 5**
REFLECTIVE JOURNALING

Each day, allocate 5-10 minutes in the morning for reflection and creating daily affirmations, followed by another 5-10 minutes in the evening to review and evaluate your day's decisions and experiences.

EVENING JOURNALING

Decision Points (throughout the day): Identify at least three moments in the day you made decisions automatically.

_____
_____
_____
_____
_____
_____

Deliberate Choices (1-2 minutes each): For each identified decision point, consider what options (if any) you may have.

_____
_____
_____
_____
_____
_____

Reflection(s) (5-10 minutes): Conclude your day by reflecting on your choices, outcomes, desired changes, and what was intentional/unintentional.

_____
_____
_____
_____
_____

WEEK 10 | **"THE CHOICE IS MINE"** | DAY 6
REFLECTIVE JOURNALING

Each day, allocate 5-10 minutes in the morning for reflection and creating daily affirmations, followed by another 5-10 minutes in the evening to review and evaluate your day's decisions and experiences.

MORNING JOURNALING

Reflection: What do you hope to experience or achiever today?

_____
_____
_____
_____
_____
_____
_____

TODAY'S AFFIRMATION(S)

Write down this prompt and complete the sentence in the space provided below: "YOUR NAME" I love you today because...

_____
_____
_____

WEEK 10 — **"THE CHOICE IS MINE"** — DAY 6
REFLECTIVE JOURNALING

Each day, allocate 5-10 minutes in the morning for reflection and creating daily affirmations, followed by another 5-10 minutes in the evening to review and evaluate your day's decisions and experiences.

EVENING JOURNALING

Decision Points (throughout the day): Identify at least three moments in the day you made decisions automatically.

_____
_____
_____
_____
_____

Deliberate Choices (1-2 minutes each): For each identified decision point, consider what options (if any) you may have.

_____
_____
_____
_____
_____

Reflection(s) (5-10 minutes): Conclude your day by reflecting on your choices, outcomes, desired changes, and what was intentional/unintentional.

_____
_____
_____
_____

WEEK 10 — **"THE CHOICE IS MINE"** — DAY 7
REFLECTIVE JOURNALING

Each day, allocate 5-10 minutes in the morning for reflection and creating daily affirmations, followed by another 5-10 minutes in the evening to review and evaluate your day's decisions and experiences.

MORNING JOURNALING

Reflection: What do you hope to experience or achiever today?

_____
_____
_____
_____
_____
_____
_____

TODAY'S AFFIRMATION(S)

_____   _____
_____   _____
_____   _____
_____   _____
_____   _____
_____   _____
_____   _____

Write down this prompt and complete the sentence in the space provided below: "YOUR NAME" I love you today because...

_____
_____
_____

WEEK 10   **"THE CHOICE IS MINE"**   DAY 7
REFLECTIVE JOURNALING

Each day, allocate 5-10 minutes in the morning for reflection and creating daily affirmations, followed by another 5-10 minutes in the evening to review and evaluate your day's decisions and experiences.

EVENING JOURNALING

Decision Points (throughout the day): Identify at least three moments in the day you made decisions automatically.

_____
_____
_____
_____
_____
_____

Deliberate Choices (1-2 minutes each): For each identified decision point, consider what options (if any) you may have.

_____
_____
_____
_____
_____
_____

Reflection(s) (5-10 minutes): Conclude your day by reflecting on your choices, outcomes, desired changes, and what was intentional/unintentional.

_____
_____
_____
_____

CHAPTER 11

How to Confront Fear?

Andy:

Andy was caught in a paralyzing paradox: the fear of fear itself.

A compassionate individual with a sharp intellect, he found himself wrestling with a deep anxiety that stemmed not from specific external threats but from his internal dialogue around fear. He had internalized the notion that fear and anxiety were character flaws to be eradicated, and in doing so, he had entered a self-defeating cycle.

Despite his capabilities, Andy was stunted, both personally and professionally. He spent his energy not on action but on avoidance of anything that could trigger fear or reveal his perceived imperfections. He was like a plane in a holding pattern, burning fuel but never landing, never reaching a destination, caught in an endless loop of *what-ifs*.

In therapy, Andy and I began to unpack these fears. We explored the collateral of his choices – to remain in constant suspension or take the risk of landing and living. We acknowledged that the plane must come down eventually, and we pondered whether it would be through a crash or a deliberate act of courage.

Together, we started the work of reframing his relationship with fear. Instead of viewing fear as an enemy, we began to consider how it might be a motivator, a part of the human condition that could not be excised but could be understood and harnessed. We slowly worked toward embracing the possibility beyond fear – the possibility of choice, action, and, ultimately, growth.

Andy's journey is ongoing, a testament to the human struggle with the unknown and the power of choice in the face of inevitable change. The goal for Andy is not to eliminate fear but to learn to fly with it, to choose his path, and to land the plane by choice, embracing whatever may come with the knowledge that he is the pilot of his own life.

The After Session:

"If I waited until I had all my ducks in a row, I'd never cross the street. Sometimes you gotta gather up what you've got and make a run for it" – Judge Lynn Toler.

What would be the result of a life acknowledging our fears? Knowing that we will always have a few, which can be used to motivate or destroy, even if we have never gotten rid of them. Anxiety can manifest in several ways and become problematic when we least expect it. Some forms of anxiety are rooted in fear of the unknown:

- What reaction would we get if we said, *"I love you?"*
- What would life be like if we allowed ourselves to be loved?
- What would it mean to acknowledge that someone didn't show up for us when we expected it?
- What opportunities could open up if we were more assertive at work?
- What pain would result from telling a parent that we wish they protected us when our first sexual experience was forced?

What if we understood that all of life's questions and possible answers have some collateral? Would we go for it, or keep wondering? The inability to express our feelings or choosing to prioritize everyone's needs above our own causes harm in one way. The possible fallout from no longer doing so could harm us in another. As a result, we sometimes find ourselves stuck in this holding pattern. We know what causes anxiety but are too afraid to change it because change itself is anxiety-provoking.

So, we continue to navigate a never-ending cycle of unanswered questions and unspoken truths for fear of what might be.

Fear of the possibility.

If we're pilots navigating the plane of life, we might end up flying a route where all ground communication is lost. We're in it all alone. We'll never get the *"all clear for landing."* So, at first, it's logical to fly in a holding pattern, circling until we get a sign for a safe landing.

But what if we never see a sign or run out of fuel before the message comes? The one thing we know for sure is that the plane eventually MUST COME DOWN. Will it be a crash landing or an act of bravery to try and land without knowing the result?

In life, it may seem that there are no options. What is certain is that even if we choose to keep circling, a landing is inevitable. If we break the holding pattern without the "all clear," we might get the same result, but there is also the possibility of a safer landing. Will we land by choice or force?

It's similar in our interactions with loved ones, coworkers, and ourselves. Often, we avoid asking for what we need because we fear the answer might be "no." This fear prevents us from addressing needs that are already unmet. We tell ourselves that pursuing our needs could lead to disaster, choosing instead to wait and hope others will notice and choose to meet our needs – something they might never do. Ultimately, this waiting can lead us to crash and burn. This is when we fear what we already have but are convincing ourselves that speaking somehow will be worse. See the pattern?

THE INEVITABLE DESCENT

Andy's journey narrated the inner turmoil of a person wrestling with his own perceptions of fear, viewed through a lens of avoidance and imperfection. Andy's journey reflects the broader human condition – a testament to the challenges and triumphs encountered in the pursuit of personal growth.

In his therapeutic sessions, Andy learned to redefine his relationship with fear, not as a debilitating force but as a motivating ally. The discussions revealed the nuanced dynamics of anxiety, the constant "what-ifs," and the paralysis brought on by the fear of possible outcomes. These sessions provided Andy with the tools to navigate his fears, propelling him from a state of endless circling to preparing for a deliberate landing.

The metaphor of the plane, used throughout our sessions, provided an objective symbolism of Andy's situation. Initially trapped in a holding pattern by his own doubts and fears, Andy began to understand that the only way to move forward was to take control and initiate the landing himself, irrespective of the uncertainties that lie ahead. This shift in perspective is crucial – not just for Andy but for anyone reading his story. It teaches us that while fear is an inevitable part of life, it does not have to define our entire journey.

I was able to relate these insights to the broader human experience, highlighting the universality of these struggles. Judge Lynn Toler's powerful quote reminds us that waiting for perfect conditions is an exercise in futility. Instead, acknowledging our fears, understanding their origins and potential impacts, and choosing to act despite them can lead to significant personal breakthroughs.

Andy's ongoing journey underscores a strong reminder: The act of landing, fraught with unknowns, is not merely about ending the flight but about embracing the possibilities that come after. Whether through force or choice, each decision to address our fears brings us closer to understanding ourselves and mastering the art of living courageously.

We are invited to reflect on our own lives through Andy's journey. Are we, too, in a holding pattern, waiting for signs that may never come? Or are we ready to take the controls, brave the descent, and land wherever it may lead us, armed with the wisdom that whatever happens, we have the power to rise again?

WEEK 11   **"CONFRONTING THE HOLDING PATTERN"**   DATE:
REFLECTIVE JOURNALING

This exercise aims to help confront fears and the holding pattern life has become due to the fear of fear itself. It's designed to expose us to the fears we're avoiding gradually and to practice making active choices rather than being paralyzed by 'what-ifs.'

Each day, reflect on something that might be holding us back and think of the smallest possible step, challenge, measure, or barrier in the overall goal of confronting this fear
(incremental steps).

Identifying Fears:
Each day, identify one specific fear contributing to your 'holding pattern.' It might be the fear of rejection, failure, or vulnerability. Write this fear down in the journal.

Small Exposure:
Plan a small, manageable action that confronts this fear in a very controlled way. For example, if the fear is of rejection, the action might be complimenting a stranger, opening himself up to any response.

Reflection Before Action:
Before you take action, reflect on what you're feeling. What is the fear telling you? What is the worst that could happen, and how likely is it?

Taking Action:
Execute the planned action. You must fully experience the moment and whatever feelings arise during the interaction.

Post-Action Reflection:
After the action, write down what happened. How did you feel before, during, and after? Did the reality match the fear? Reflect on how it feels to have taken control, even in a small way.

Exploring Collateral:
Consider the 'collateral' of both action and inaction. What are the consequences of avoiding fear versus confronting it? How does each path align with how you want to live your life?

WEEK 11 — **"CONFRONTING THE HOLDING PATTERN"** — DAY 1
REFLECTIVE JOURNALING

Each day, allocate 5-10 minutes in the morning for reflection on fear and one small step that you can take to overcome it over time. Then, follow by another 5-10 minutes in the evening to review and evaluate your action to further confront what binds you.

MORNING JOURNALING

Identifying Fears: What binds or holds you back due to fear or the anxiety of not being enough?

_____
_____
_____
_____

Small Exposure: Plan a small, manageable action that you can take today to confront this fear in a very controlled way.

_____
_____
_____
_____

Reflection Before Action: Before you take action, reflect on what you're feeling.

_____
_____
_____
_____

Taking Action: Execute the planned action, practice the small measure today by (identify the action).

_____
_____
_____

WEEK 11   **"CONFRONTING THE HOLDING PATTERN"**   DAY 1
REFLECTIVE JOURNALING

Each day, allocate 5-10 minutes in the morning for reflection on fear and one small step that you can take to overcome it over time. Then, follow by another 5-10 minutes in the evening to review and evaluate your action to further confront what binds you.

EVENING JOURNALING

Post-Action Reflection: What happened? How did you feel before, during, and after? Did the reality match the fear? Or, what (if anything) stopped you from taking the small step?

WEEK 11   **"CONFRONTING THE HOLDING PATTERN"**   `DAY 2`
REFLECTIVE JOURNALING

Each day, allocate 5-10 minutes in the morning for reflection on fear and one small step that you can take to overcome it over time. Then, follow by another 5-10 minutes in the evening to review and evaluate your action to further confront what binds you.

MORNING JOURNALING

Identifying Fears: What binds or holds you back due to fear or the anxiety of not being enough?

_____
_____
_____
_____

Small Exposure: Plan a small, manageable action that you can take today to confront this fear in a very controlled way.

_____
_____
_____
_____

Reflection Before Action: Before you take action, reflect on what you're feeling.

_____
_____
_____
_____

Taking Action: Execute the planned action, practice the small measure today by (identify the action).

_____
_____
_____

WEEK 11	**"CONFRONTING THE HOLDING PATTERN"** DAY 2
	REFLECTIVE JOURNALING

Each day, allocate 5-10 minutes in the morning for reflection on fear and one small step that you can take to overcome it over time. Then, follow by another 5-10 minutes in the evening to review and evaluate your action to further confront what binds you.

EVENING JOURNALING

Post-Action Reflection: What happened? How did you feel before, during, and after? Did the reality match the fear? Or, what (if anything) stopped you from taking the small step?

WEEK 11   **"CONFRONTING THE HOLDING PATTERN"**   **DAY 3**
REFLECTIVE JOURNALING

Each day, allocate 5-10 minutes in the morning for reflection on fear and one small step that you can take to overcome it over time. Then, follow by another 5-10 minutes in the evening to review and evaluate your action to further confront what binds you.

MORNING JOURNALING

Identifying Fears: What binds or holds you back due to fear or the anxiety of not being enough?

_____
_____
_____
_____

Small Exposure: Plan a small, manageable action that you can take today to confront this fear in a very controlled way.

_____
_____
_____
_____

Reflection Before Action: Before you take action, reflect on what you're feeling.

_____
_____
_____
_____

Taking Action: Execute the planned action, practice the small measure today by (identify the action).

_____
_____
_____

| WEEK 11 | **"CONFRONTING THE HOLDING PATTERN"** | DAY 3 |

REFLECTIVE JOURNALING

Each day, allocate 5-10 minutes in the morning for reflection on fear and one small step that you can take to overcome it over time. Then, follow by another 5-10 minutes in the evening to review and evaluate your action to further confront what binds you.

EVENING JOURNALING

Post-Action Reflection: What happened? How did you feel before, during, and after? Did the reality match the fear? Or, what (if anything) stopped you from taking the small step?

WEEK 11   **"CONFRONTING THE HOLDING PATTERN"**   **DAY 4**
REFLECTIVE JOURNALING

Each day, allocate 5-10 minutes in the morning for reflection on fear and one small step that you can take to overcome it over time. Then, follow by another 5-10 minutes in the evening to review and evaluate your action to further confront what binds you.

MORNING JOURNALING

Identifying Fears: What binds or holds you back due to fear or the anxiety of not being enough?

_____
_____
_____
_____

Small Exposure: Plan a small, manageable action that you can take today to confront this fear in a very controlled way.

_____
_____
_____
_____

Reflection Before Action: Before you take action, reflect on what you're feeling.

_____
_____
_____
_____

Taking Action: Execute the planned action, practice the small measure today by (identify the action).

_____
_____
_____
_____

WEEK 11   **"CONFRONTING THE HOLDING PATTERN"**   DAY 4
REFLECTIVE JOURNALING

Each day, allocate 5-10 minutes in the morning for reflection on fear and one small step that you can take to overcome it over time. Then, follow by another 5-10 minutes in the evening to review and evaluate your action to further confront what binds you.

EVENING JOURNALING

Post-Action Reflection: What happened? How did you feel before, during, and after? Did the reality match the fear? Or, what (if anything) stopped you from taking the small step?

_____
_____
_____
_____
_____
_____
_____
_____
_____
_____
_____
_____
_____
_____
_____
_____
_____
_____
_____

WEEK 11   **"CONFRONTING THE HOLDING PATTERN"**   DAY 5
REFLECTIVE JOURNALING

Each day, allocate 5-10 minutes in the morning for reflection on fear and one small step that you can take to overcome it over time. Then, follow by another 5-10 minutes in the evening to review and evaluate your action to further confront what binds you.

MORNING JOURNALING

Identifying Fears: What binds or holds you back due to fear or the anxiety of not being enough?

_____
_____
_____
_____

Small Exposure: Plan a small, manageable action that you can take today to confront this fear in a very controlled way.

_____
_____
_____
_____

Reflection Before Action: Before you take action, reflect on what you're feeling.

_____
_____
_____
_____

Taking Action: Execute the planned action, practice the small measure today by (identify the action).

_____
_____
_____

| WEEK 11 | **"CONFRONTING THE HOLDING PATTERN"** | DAY 5 |

REFLECTIVE JOURNALING

Each day, allocate 5-10 minutes in the morning for reflection on fear and one small step that you can take to overcome it over time. Then, follow by another 5-10 minutes in the evening to review and evaluate your action to further confront what binds you.

EVENING JOURNALING

Post-Action Reflection: What happened? How did you feel before, during, and after? Did the reality match the fear? Or, what (if anything) stopped you from taking the small step?

WEEK 11   **"CONFRONTING THE HOLDING PATTERN"**   DAY 6
REFLECTIVE JOURNALING

Each day, allocate 5-10 minutes in the morning for reflection on fear and one small step that you can take to overcome it over time. Then, follow by another 5-10 minutes in the evening to review and evaluate your action to further confront what binds you.

MORNING JOURNALING

Identifying Fears: What binds or holds you back due to fear or the anxiety of not being enough?

_____
_____
_____
_____

Small Exposure: Plan a small, manageable action that you can take today to confront this fear in a very controlled way.

_____
_____
_____
_____

Reflection Before Action: Before you take action, reflect on what you're feeling.

_____
_____
_____
_____

Taking Action: Execute the planned action, practice the small measure today by (identify the action).

_____
_____
_____

WEEK 11	**"CONFRONTING THE HOLDING PATTERN"**	DAY 6

REFLECTIVE JOURNALING

Each day, allocate 5-10 minutes in the morning for reflection on fear and one small step that you can take to overcome it over time. Then, follow by another 5-10 minutes in the evening to review and evaluate your action to further confront what binds you.

EVENING JOURNALING

Post-Action Reflection: What happened? How did you feel before, during, and after? Did the reality match the fear? Or, what (if anything) stopped you from taking the small step?

WEEK 11 — "CONFRONTING THE HOLDING PATTERN" — DAY 7
REFLECTIVE JOURNALING

Each day, allocate 5-10 minutes in the morning for reflection on fear and one small step that you can take to overcome it over time. Then, follow by another 5-10 minutes in the evening to review and evaluate your action to further confront what binds you.

MORNING JOURNALING

Identifying Fears: What binds or holds you back due to fear or the anxiety of not being enough?

_____
_____
_____
_____

Small Exposure: Plan a small, manageable action that you can take today to confront this fear in a very controlled way.

_____
_____
_____
_____

Reflection Before Action: Before you take action, reflect on what you're feeling.

_____
_____
_____
_____

Taking Action: Execute the planned action, practice the small measure today by (identify the action).

_____
_____
_____

WEEK 11   **"CONFRONTING THE HOLDING PATTERN"**   DAY 7
REFLECTIVE JOURNALING

Each day, allocate 5-10 minutes in the morning for reflection on fear and one small step that you can take to overcome it over time. Then, follow by another 5-10 minutes in the evening to review and evaluate your action to further confront what binds you.

EVENING JOURNALING

Post-Action Reflection: What happened? How did you feel before, during, and after? Did the reality match the fear? Or, what (if anything) stopped you from taking the small step?

CHAPTER 12

Faith, Belief, and Knowing

Lawrence:

Lawrence initially came into my office at his mother's recommendation. Following a breakup, the family noticed something was different.

Lawrence's understanding of himself was impacted by the relationship he no longer had. He had little self-esteem, and his view of himself seemed skewed by his understanding that his girlfriend didn't choose him. And, because he wasn't chosen, it meant he wasn't good enough. The notion that Lawrence wasn't good enough was a familiar message he picked up through many experiences growing up:

- Reactions to him expressing his religious beliefs.
- Realizing things he didn't like about his body.
- Experiencing exclusion from peer groups during social activities.
- Feeling overlooked in dynamics where others received more attention.
- Facing consistent criticism rather than encouragement in his creative endeavors.

What he did have a lot of was faith. From the first day we met, Lawrence understood that he wanted to get better – and could get better – because he knew that if he kept working on himself, he eventually would. The only question was how, not *if*.

Throughout our sessions, Lawrence was ready to dive into any technique, explore any life experience, and walk through any challenge. He was determined to understand and change the narrative he had about himself. We worked on building his self-esteem by identifying his strengths, acknowledging his accomplishments, and addressing the negative self-perception from his past experiences and the recent breakup. Our therapy focused on reconstructing his self-identity independently of others' perceptions or actions towards him. Lawrence learned to appreciate his worth and to understand that his value is not contingent on someone else's approval, acceptance, or choice to be with him.

He also began to practice self-compassion, understanding that his feelings of rejection and inadequacy were a part of his experience but not defining. With each session, Lawrence became more adept at recognizing and challenging his negative thought patterns and, more importantly, envisioning a future where he felt confident and self-assured.

Lawrence's journey is ongoing, but his progress is evident. He is a testament to the power of belief in self-love, aiding in self-improvement, and the willingness to engage in the challenging work of personal growth and knowing certain truths about ourselves.

The After Session:

Faith – not in the religious sense, but the simple belief that things will get better. It's often understood to be the complete trust and confidence in someone or something.

Two types of people tend to walk into my office for therapy: those who *know* and those who aren't sure. The *knowers* believe and understand certain things to be true, while those who aren't sure use hope – the desire and wanting for something to happen. Maybe the hope will lead them to faith, belief, and knowing. But, knowing does not require or have a place for hoping. However, hope can help process the foundational elements of faith and belief to eventually get to the point of knowing something to be true.

Those who know understand that whatever they're going through will eventually end – whether it's their time with me, the office, our work, finding another therapist, or talking to friends. Something will have a collateral impact, and the outcome can never be static – things will not be the same. They know if they move forward, they're moving. Period. The *knowers* understand that if they assert change and take on the work to improve themselves and their environment, they will eventually achieve their goals.

Others come to my office for *hope*. There is no fundamental difference between these two types of people, except one person knows they'll get better, while the other hopes they will.

I often remind the *hopers* that, as a therapist, I can do nothing to make them feel better. It's up to them to take what they are given and apply it as best as possible. Therapists provide tools, interpret what we see (the information shared by the person in the room, whether they are honest or not), and shed light on what has been scientifically or experientially proven to address the topic.

Applying the principles we discuss comes naturally to those who know they will improve. They allow their belief in the process and themselves to guide their progress towards their goals. Conversely, I spend additional time with others to help them build motivation and to understand the importance of change. For those who expect to improve, the protocol is just one of many tools available to evaluate together whether it's the right approach for their need. However, those who lack knowledge of their change often feel as if there are no tools available at all, and any setback with the treatment or protocol used reinforces their belief that they won't get better. We frequently need to challenge these negative self-conceptions and their understanding of what life and self can be beyond mere hopes.

This perspective adjustment is crucial, especially for those who are first-generation or those pursuing unprecedented dreams within their environments. The task is to redefine what's possible before we can even utilize the tools necessary to build the life they envision. The journey of hope can be exhausting, particularly when it involves blazing a new trail – like cutting through dense forests or laying new concrete paths that have never been trodden. It allows one to believe the exhaustion of creating a path means they won't be able to begin the journey on it once the path is made.

Often, we overlook the progress we've made, exhausting ourselves physically and emotionally. It's crucial to interpret these feelings as fatigue and signs of change, big or small. Sometimes, acknowledging a setback or recognizing negative shifts in our behavior or thinking **is a sign of progress**. At the end of the day, if we weren't evolving or aware that there's more to achieve, we wouldn't recognize a setback at all. Falling off the proverbial horse serves as a reminder that there's more work to be done. If we were stagnant in our growth, we wouldn't even realize we had fallen. Each challenge is an opportunity to reaffirm our commitment to growth and change.

Instead of merely continuing to hope, it's essential to use the evidence of what has been achieved – or the acknowledgment of what hasn't – to foster a fundamental understanding and conviction that improvement is possible, better yet, inevitable.

One thing I can say with certainty – something I rarely do because so few things in life are certain – is that *knowing* profoundly impacts the care of the mind, body, soul, and emotions; **knowing makes all the difference.**

KNOWLEDGE FOR TRANSFORMATION

The intricacies of Lawrence's therapeutic journey mirror a broader narrative where self-awareness and intentional growth lay the foundation for the road toward healing and self-acceptance. Lawrence's experience, as narrated through our sessions, underscores the impact of embracing one's worth independent of external validation. This shift from seeking approval to affirming one's own value is a powerful stride toward emotional freedom and reconciliation.

Throughout our work together, Lawrence exemplified the transition from hoping for better days to knowing they are achievable, laying a foundation for others to understand that the essence of therapy transcends mere conversation – it is an active, lived experience of reconstructing one's identity and values in the face of past adversities. As his therapist, observing Lawrence's journey from a seeker of validation to a knower of his intrinsic worth has been both a privilege and a profound learning experience.

Lawrence's journey is a beacon for those embarking on similar paths. It reiterates the importance of recognizing our internal narratives and the power we hold to redefine them. Lawrence's story is a reminder that the path to self-improvement is iterative and dynamic, shaped by both setbacks and victories.

In moving forward, Lawrence's ongoing journey has inspired me, and hopefully, others, who find themselves in the throes of self-doubt and external dependence. His transformation from hope to knowledge illuminates the therapeutic process as a roadmap for profound personal change, where the ultimate success is not just in overcoming but in **becoming**.

Lawrence's evolution from hope to certainty offers a compelling narrative of the healing power of knowing oneself deeply and truly – a narrative that continues to unfold with each step he takes into a future he now **knows** he can shape.

| PRACTICE | **"THE PATH TO KNOWING"**
REFLECTIVE DIALOGUE | DATE: |

Reflect on the following questions to solidify your journey from hope to knowing:

Success story/stories: What successes have I had in the past that prove I can overcome challenges?

_____
_____
_____
_____
_____
_____
_____
_____
_____
_____
_____
_____
_____
_____
_____
_____
_____
_____
_____
_____
_____
_____
_____
_____
_____

PRACTICE **"THE PATH TO KNOWING"** DATE
REFLECTIVE DIALOGUE

Reflect on the following questions to solidify your journey from hope to knowing:

Looking Ahead: What are the next steps in my journey toward knowing?

_____
_____
_____
_____
_____
_____
_____
_____
_____
_____

How will I apply what I've learned about my experiences and current place in life to new challenges?

_____
_____
_____
_____
_____
_____
_____
_____

WEEK 12   **"THE PATH TO KNOWING"**   **DAY 1**
REFLECTIVE JOURNALING

Each day, allocate 5-10 minutes in the morning for reflection, followed by another 5-10 minutes in the evening to review and evaluate what it all means.

Mindset Shift: Begin each morning by stating a positive affirmation about the belief in change. For example, "I am moving forward and improving every day."

_____
_____
_____
_____

Reflection on Past Successes: Write about past situations where you overcame difficulties. Reflect on the strengths and strategies that helped you succeed.

_____
_____
_____
_____
_____
_____

Setting Intention: Set a clear intention for the day that aligns with your goals. This intention should be a stepping stone toward your larger goal, or measurable step toward the goal.

Today I intend to _____
_____
_____

Daily Action: Identify one action you can take daily that moves you towards your goal. It could be researching a topic, practicing a skill, or reaching out for support (*I will do_____ to fulfill today's intention*)

_____
_____
_____

WEEK 12   **"THE PATH TO KNOWING"**   DAY 1
REFLECTIVE JOURNALING

Each day, allocate 5-10 minutes in the morning for reflection, followed by another 5-10 minutes in the evening to review and evaluate what it all means.

EVENING JOURNALING

Evening Reflection: Each evening, reflect on the day's actions and intentions. Write about what worked, what didn't, and how it felt to take proactive steps towards your goal.

WEEK 12   **"THE PATH TO KNOWING"**   DAY 2
REFLECTIVE JOURNALING

Each day, allocate 5-10 minutes in the morning for reflection, followed by another 5-10 minutes in the evening to review and evaluate what it all means.

Mindset Shift: Begin each morning by stating a positive affirmation about the belief in change. For example, "I am moving forward and improving every day."

_____

_____

_____

_____

Reflection on Past Successes: Write about past situations where you overcame difficulties. Reflect on the strengths and strategies that helped you succeed.

_____

_____

_____

_____

_____

Setting Intention: Set a clear intention for the day that aligns with your goals. This intention should be a stepping stone toward your larger goal, or measurable step toward the goal.

Today I intend to _____

_____

_____

Daily Action: Identify one action you can take daily that moves you towards your goal. It could be researching a topic, practicing a skill, or reaching out for support *(I will do_____ to fulfill today's intention)*

_____

_____

_____

WEEK 12 — **"THE PATH TO KNOWING"** — DAY 2
REFLECTIVE JOURNALING

Each day, allocate 5-10 minutes in the morning for reflection, followed by another 5-10 minutes in the evening to review and evaluate what it all means.

EVENING JOURNALING

Evening Reflection: Each evening, reflect on the day's actions and intentions. Write about what worked, what didn't, and how it felt to take proactive steps towards your goal.

| WEEK 12 | **"THE PATH TO KNOWING"**
REFLECTIVE JOURNALING | DAY 3 |

Each day, allocate 5-10 minutes in the morning for reflection, followed by another 5-10 minutes in the evening to review and evaluate what it all means.

Mindset Shift: Begin each morning by stating a positive affirmation about the belief in change. For example, "I am moving forward and improving every day."

_____

_____

_____

_____

Reflection on Past Successes: Write about past situations where you overcame difficulties. Reflect on the strengths and strategies that helped you succeed.

_____

_____

_____

_____

_____

_____

Setting Intention: Set a clear intention for the day that aligns with your goals. This intention should be a stepping stone toward your larger goal, or measurable step toward the goal.

Today I intend to _____

_____

_____

Daily Action: Identify one action you can take daily that moves you towards your goal. It could be researching a topic, practicing a skill, or reaching out for support *(I will do_____ to fulfill today's intention)*

_____

_____

_____

WEEK 12   **"THE PATH TO KNOWING"**   DAY 3
REFLECTIVE JOURNALING

Each day, allocate 5-10 minutes in the morning for reflection, followed by another 5-10 minutes in the evening to review and evaluate what it all means.

EVENING JOURNALING

Evening Reflection: Each evening, reflect on the day's actions and intentions. Write about what worked, what didn't, and how it felt to take proactive steps towards your goal.

_____
_____
_____
_____
_____
_____
_____
_____
_____
_____
_____
_____
_____
_____
_____
_____
_____
_____
_____
_____

| WEEK 12 | **"THE PATH TO KNOWING"** | DAY 4 |

REFLECTIVE JOURNALING

Each day, allocate 5-10 minutes in the morning for reflection, followed by another 5-10 minutes in the evening to review and evaluate what it all means.

Mindset Shift: Begin each morning by stating a positive affirmation about the belief in change. For example, "I am moving forward and improving every day."

_____
_____
_____
_____

Reflection on Past Successes: Write about past situations where you overcame difficulties. Reflect on the strengths and strategies that helped you succeed.

_____
_____
_____
_____
_____
_____

Setting Intention: Set a clear intention for the day that aligns with your goals. This intention should be a stepping stone toward your larger goal, or measurable step toward the goal.

Today I intend to _____
_____
_____

Daily Action: Identify one action you can take daily that moves you towards your goal. It could be researching a topic, practicing a skill, or reaching out for support (I will do_____ to fulfill today's intention)

_____
_____
_____

WEEK 12   **"THE PATH TO KNOWING"**   DAY 4
REFLECTIVE JOURNALING

Each day, allocate 5-10 minutes in the morning for reflection, followed by another 5-10 minutes in the evening to review and evaluate what it all means.

EVENING JOURNALING

Evening Reflection: Each evening, reflect on the day's actions and intentions. Write about what worked, what didn't, and how it felt to take proactive steps towards your goal.

WEEK 12   **"THE PATH TO KNOWING"**   **DAY 5**
REFLECTIVE JOURNALING

Each day, allocate 5-10 minutes in the morning for reflection, followed by another 5-10 minutes in the evening to review and evaluate what it all means.

Mindset Shift: Begin each morning by stating a positive affirmation about the belief in change. For example, "I am moving forward and improving every day."

_____

_____

_____

_____

Reflection on Past Successes: Write about past situations where you overcame difficulties. Reflect on the strengths and strategies that helped you succeed.

_____

_____

_____

_____

_____

_____

Setting Intention: Set a clear intention for the day that aligns with your goals. This intention should be a stepping stone toward your larger goal, or measurable step toward the goal.

Today I intend to _____

_____

_____

Daily Action: Identify one action you can take daily that moves you towards your goal. It could be researching a topic, practicing a skill, or reaching out for support (*I will do_____ to fulfill today's intention*)

_____

_____

_____

WEEK 12   **"THE PATH TO KNOWING"**   **DAY 5**
REFLECTIVE JOURNALING

Each day, allocate 5-10 minutes in the morning for reflection, followed by another 5-10 minutes in the evening to review and evaluate what it all means.

EVENING JOURNALING

Evening Reflection: Each evening, reflect on the day's actions and intentions. Write about what worked, what didn't, and how it felt to take proactive steps towards your goal.

WEEK 12   **"THE PATH TO KNOWING"**   **DAY 6**
REFLECTIVE JOURNALING

Each day, allocate 5-10 minutes in the morning for reflection, followed by another 5-10 minutes in the evening to review and evaluate what it all means.

Mindset Shift: Begin each morning by stating a positive affirmation about the belief in change. For example, "I am moving forward and improving every day."

_____
_____
_____
_____

Reflection on Past Successes: Write about past situations where you overcame difficulties. Reflect on the strengths and strategies that helped you succeed.

_____
_____
_____
_____
_____
_____

Setting Intention: Set a clear intention for the day that aligns with your goals. This intention should be a stepping stone toward your larger goal, or measurable step toward the goal.

Today I intend to _____
_____
_____

Daily Action: Identify one action you can take daily that moves you towards your goal. It could be researching a topic, practicing a skill, or reaching out for support *(I will do_____ to fulfill today's intention)*

_____
_____
_____

WEEK 12   **"THE PATH TO KNOWING"**   DAY 6
REFLECTIVE JOURNALING

Each day, allocate 5-10 minutes in the morning for reflection, followed by another 5-10 minutes in the evening to review and evaluate what it all means.

EVENING JOURNALING

Evening Reflection: Each evening, reflect on the day's actions and intentions. Write about what worked, what didn't, and how it felt to take proactive steps towards your goal.

WEEK 12   **"THE PATH TO KNOWING"**   DAY 7
REFLECTIVE JOURNALING

Each day, allocate 5-10 minutes in the morning for reflection, followed by another 5-10 minutes in the evening to review and evaluate what it all means.

Mindset Shift: Begin each morning by stating a positive affirmation about the belief in change. For example, "I am moving forward and improving every day."

_____
_____
_____
_____

Reflection on Past Successes: Write about past situations where you overcame difficulties. Reflect on the strengths and strategies that helped you succeed.

_____
_____
_____
_____
_____
_____

Setting Intention: Set a clear intention for the day that aligns with your goals. This intention should be a stepping stone toward your larger goal, or measurable step toward the goal.

Today I intend to _____
_____
_____

Daily Action: Identify one action you can take daily that moves you towards your goal. It could be researching a topic, practicing a skill, or reaching out for support (*I will do_____ to fulfill today's intention*)

_____
_____
_____

WEEK 12   **"THE PATH TO KNOWING"**   **DAY 7**
REFLECTIVE JOURNALING

Each day, allocate 5-10 minutes in the morning for reflection, followed by another 5-10 minutes in the evening to review and evaluate what it all means.

EVENING JOURNALING

Evening Reflection: Each evening, reflect on the day's actions and intentions. Write about what worked, what didn't, and how it felt to take proactive steps towards your goal.

_____
_____
_____
_____
_____
_____
_____
_____
_____
_____
_____
_____
_____
_____
_____
_____
_____
_____

WEEK 12   **"THE PATH TO KNOWING"**   DAY 7
REFLECTIVE JOURNALING

End-of-Week Review
At the end of the week, review your daily reflections. Look for patterns and growth points.

Review of the Week: How have your actions reinforced your beliefs and progress?

___

Adapting Tools: When you encounter an obstacle or a setback, reflect on the tools and strategies you've used. How can you adapt these tools to address the current challenge?

___

NOTES

DATE:

NOTES

DATE:

NOTES

DATE:

NOTES

DATE:

Acknowledgments

One individual has not only changed my life but has also contributed to its creation: Mommy, you epitomize the essence of God's word and the transformative depth of love. This workbook, and most of what I do, is because of who you are. All I have been, am, and ever will be is because **you are**. Your strength, love, and existence in my life can't be measured. It's impossible to comprehend how much you have done for me and all you have meant for me and my life. I love you, always.

I must pay homage to the multitude of black women in my life, who, through their love, care, concern, and even discord, have continually shifted my life in a positive direction. Whether we were lovers, friends, or in between, you have contributed to my healing. This might even seem problematic. Far too often, women – particularly women of color – are left carrying the emotional baggage of broken men. I pray that at some point, through our intertwined lives, I have given you some equivalent – if not more – of what you've given me. If not, hold me accountable, teach me, lead me, and expect more of me.

My brothas, specifically George and James. Man, there have been so many complicated and interesting times we've been through. Although we don't speak every day, I always know that you want the best for me and have continually pushed me to be better through direct encouragement or through my seeing and admiring the exemplary men you have become for your children and family.

I would be remiss not to directly acknowledge a few individuals who helped make this publication and this journey possible. In no specific order: Cory, my editor. Seriously, this has been the most extended process for anything I have done that wasn't required or mandatory. As often as I started and stopped, found other projects, or flat-out avoided doing this altogether, a substantial part of this being started and finished is because of you. Donavon, thanks for bringing my tangential ideas to life with the cover and having the patience to bring my thoughts to life through your artistic expression. Natasha, thanks for always expecting more of me. Satmah, thank you for always listening, even when I may be a bit manic, never saying any idea was ever too big, and always asking what's next. Claudine, thank you for always telling me exactly when I think or see myself as too small. Gabriela, on the late nights or early mornings, if you weren't there to answer or hold space, I still wonder where I'd be. You've blessed me more than you know. Nicole and Lakesha, I feel so safe knowing you both are in the world and will always have my back. Nothing I've ever done has sounded crazy, and you've always inspired me. Tenaya, you continue to be my teacher with every passing day. Living fully is always tricky, and you make it look easy. Brandy, you've always been there, and knowing you will always be allows me to continue moving forward. For this, I thank you. My siblings, Melecia, Felecia, Moesha, and Taniesha, I hope that you can always feel my love.

To my son, Warren, no words can express how much I love you. Nothing can separate you from my love.

Phillip J. Lewis' background is in law and clinical social work. He practices psychotherapy in Washington, D.C. and specializes in social justice counseling. Phillip's unique combination of expertise in both fields enables him to bring a comprehensive approach to addressing mental health and promoting social justice.

Edited by Cory Myer
Cover Design by Donavon Brutus

Made in the USA
Columbia, SC
11 December 2024

47805374R00124